The Gavin Ewart Show

Selected Poems 1939-1985
by Gavin Ewart

Bits Press
Cleveland

This selection from *The Collected Ewart* (1980), *The New Ewart* (1982), and *The Young Pobble's Guide to His Toes* (1985) is published by license from Century Hutchinson Limited (UK).

The drawing of the poet is by Nicola Jennings.

Cover design by Bonnie Jacobson.

Printed and bound in the U.S.A.

ISBN (cloth): 0-933248-05-9
ISBN (paper): 0-933248-06-7

f

For Margo

Contents

1982-1985

1939-1980

Audenesque for an Initiation

Don't forget the things we taught you by the broken
    water-wheel,
Don't forget the middle-classes fight much harder going
    downhill,

Don't forget that new proscriptions are being posted
    now and then,
Dr Johnson, Dr Leavis and the other Grand Old Men –

Although they've very often told us that they try to do
    their best,
Are they up to the Full Fruit Standard, would they pass
    the Spelling Test?

– Because we've got our eyes to keyholes, we know
    everything they've done,
Lecturing on minor poets. 'Literature is quite good fun.'

And if you should try to fool us, imitate them, do the
    same,
We'll refuse your dummy bullets, we've had time to take
    our aim.

We've been drinking stagnant water for some twenty
  years or more
While the politicians slowly planned a bigger reservoir.

But we've dammed a different river, the water-wheel is
  going again.
Now we've stopped designing sweaters and we've
  started in to train.

We've given up the Georgian poets, teaching dance
  bands how to croon,
Bicycling in coloured goggles underneath a pallid moon.

We've destroyed the rotting signposts, made holes in all
  the pleasure boats;
We'll pull down ancestral castles when we've time to
  swim the moats.

When we've practised we shall beat you with our Third
  or Fourth Fifteen,
In spite of Royalists on the touchline. 'Oh, well played,
  Sir!' 'Keep it clean!'

Our backs are fast as motor-cycles, all our forwards
  twenty-stone.
Each of them can score unaided, running strongly on his
  own.

Every minute scouts give signals, come reporting what
  they've seen.
'Captain Ferguson is putting.' 'Undermine the
  eighteenth green.'

Before next month we'll storm the clubhouse. Messages
  are coming through:
'Darwin, doing crossword puzzles, tries to find the
  missing clue.'

The *Times* Third Leaders are decoded, pigeon-holed for
  future use;
Tennyson has been convicted of incessant self-abuse.

13

We've been sending notes to Priestley, orange pips to
    J. C. Squire –
'Don't defend the trench you're holding.' 'Now the fat is
    in the fire.'

We've got control of all the railways and the perfume
    factories,
We're supercharged and have connection with the
    strongest batteries.

So if you feel like playing truant, remember that the
    game is up
Or you'll find that quite politely you've been sold a nasty
    pup.

We Who Were Together

We who were together shall now be apart,
Nosing our way between icebergs in this immense glacial
    world,
Different courses sailing, stamping our feet
From cold or from impatience, but with the
    remembrance of warmth
Somewhere within us and somehow remembered,
Even in this iciness never quite extinguished.
And at the mast-top the eager watcher,
Ready to shout 'Land!', draws freezing breath.

The English Wife

He had a steady hand
  And a clear eye,
He was gay, he was bland,
  And as straight as a die.

I was never frigid,
  I was never coy,
But O he has left me
  For a pretty boy,

For a gay mechanic
  Unbuttoning overalls,
More dangerous than movies
  Or the music halls.

Once he longed for me
  And my lovely bed
And in these hands have rested
  His tired head.

And the soft exertions
  Of the velvet night
Were the bold assertions
  Of my ancient right,

The language of the body,
  The sincere saying,
No winner in the game
  That we were playing.

I was significant form
  And the fabled city,
Who now am torn
  With anger and self-pity.

I was the Ideal
  And abstract beauty,
More powerful than power
  Or sense of duty.

By accident I saw them
  In the little car,
Urged with love's secrecy
  Behind the garage door.

The wind, how it did blow!
  And the rain drumming
Delayed the bitter snow,
  The crisp snow coming.

I sheltered in the doorway
  But my heart was in the storm,
While in the azure coupé
  They were warm, so warm!

With their kissing and their fingers,
  In love's aerodrome,
At the controls I left them
  And walked home.

For hours I sat in silence
  With my numbness and my pain,
But his car was stumbling westwards
  Through the bounding rain.

He drove my happiness away
  Into red Devon,
He took the brightest angels
  Out of my heaven,

Down the motorist's roads
  To the teashops and the cream
He left me sad and single
  With a sexual dream,

An unreal incubus
  And a real sorrow
Not for to-day only
  But for to-morrow.

And in the dim city
  And the aching vein
The true reality is pity
  And the pain, the pain.

Miss Twye

Miss Twye was soaping her breasts in her bath
When she heard behind her a meaning laugh
And to her amazement she discovered
A wicked man in the bathroom cupboard.

John Betjeman's Brighton

For Charles Rycroft

Lovely in the winter sunshine lies the Haslemere Hotel,
Near the Homeleigh and the Sussex, home of ex-King
  Manoel.
Lager in the West Pier Tavern, cocktails in the
  Metropole,
Who can spot Lord Alfred Douglas – not the gross and
  coarse of soul!

17

Stained our hands, our lips polluted, with a sinful
 cigarette,
We who saw 'The Dance of Love' – we are not likely to
 forget
Those moustaches and those knickers, seen through that
 machine of shame.
Palace Pier, beloved of wavelets, hushed the breath that
 bears thy name!

We remember shouting breakfasts, old men who forgot
 their teeth,
Exchanging photographs of nurses, symptoms, means
 to gain relief.
We remember that Pavilion, Moorish, with chinoiserie,
And the Ice Rink and the High Street, Fuller's layer-cake
 for tea!

Still we see those sugar-daddies flashing by in
 terraplanes,
On the Hove Lawns lonely colonels fight again their last
 campaigns;
Wickedly we drank our coffee in Sherry's where the bad
 girls go,
From the balcony we watched them bathed in purple
 light below.

O Finlandia, heavenly music, played by massed bands on
 the pier,
O those automatic palmists, how I wish that I were there!
O pin tables, Russian billiards, where the ball melodious
 clicks,
And the languid coloured postcards, bathing-girls of
 1906!

O voluptuous! O ecstatic! O that convalescent air!
In the sun those terraced houses, wonderful wonderful
 Regency Square!
There among the winds of winter we were gay in spite of
 gales,
Still a memory we cherish though the recollection pales.

Sonnet, 1940

The point where beauty and intelligence meet,
Where intersecting lines cross and divide –
Happy were I to lie between those feet
Or by that rare and warm and lovely side –
You are the centre of my moving world,
The cold ideal to which I daily move
Although iron flags of battle are unfurled –
You are not yet, though might still be, my love.
And I, before the happy tough battalions
Engulf me or the frozen seas of Norway,
Have still my dreams of cities and of dalliance,
But most of you as standing in a doorway,
Who might, though I so dissipate my life,
Be mistress or, fear of the young, a wife.

The Bofors A A Gun

Such marvellous ways to kill a man!
An 'instrument of precision', a beauty,
The well-oiled shining marvel of our day
Points an accusing finger at the sky.
– But suddenly, traversing, elevating madly,
It plunges into action, more than eager
For the steel blood of those romantic birds
That threaten all the towns and roads.
O, that man's ingenuity, in this so subtle,
In such harmonious synchronization of parts,
Should against man be turned and he complaisant,
The pheasant-shooter be himself the pheasant!

When a Beau Goes In

When a Beau goes in,
Into the drink,
It makes you think,
Because, you see, they always sink
But nobody says 'Poor lad'
Or goes about looking sad
Because, you see, it's war,
It's the unalterable law.

Although it's perfectly certain
The pilot's gone for a Burton
And the observer too
It's nothing to do with you
And if they both should go
To a land where falls no rain nor hail nor driven snow –
Here, there or anywhere,
Do you suppose *they* care?

You shouldn't cry
Or say a prayer or sigh.
In the cold sea, in the dark,
It isn't a lark
But it isn't Original Sin –
It's just a Beau going in.

Hymn to Proust

For you Time Past could not forget
    Nor alter what had been –
And Time has still its lost Odette
    And Love its Albertine.

We worship under different names
    The figures of the past,
Like characters from Henry James –
    But not designed to last.

For we know many a Charlus still
    And many a Verdurin,
Gilberte as Swann and de Forcheville,
    And M. Legrandin.

Each, an ambiguous Saint-Loup,
    Carries Françoise within,
And sex comes to its Waterloo
    In Jealousy, not Sin.

For all know Vinteuil's little phrase,
    The brilliant Balbec day,
The Méséglise and Guermantes' ways,
    The greyness of Combray.

Each one has tasted as a child
    Madeleines dipped in tea
And loves that drove the reason wild
    But set the fancy free.

Tennysonian Reflections at Barnes Bridge

The river flows before my door,
Sad with sea-gulls, mute with mud
Past Hammersmith and Castelnau,
And strung with barges at the flood.
Pink rowing girls by eight and four
Gently stroke the tide of blood.

A railway runs from side to side
And trains clank over on the hour.
The rowers strain and stretch and slide,
Hair like chrysanthemums, the flower
Of girlhood not yet opened wide,
Each happy in her virgin power.

The dying sun, the dying day
With sunlight charms suburban reaches,
The hackneyed river flows away,
And Time runs too, experience teaches,
Nor for the boring bard will stay
Or rowing girls as fresh as peaches.

Wanting Out

They're putting Man-Fix on my hair. And through the
    window
Comes a naked woman with a big whatnot. Oops! I'm
    away
To a country where the fantasies can be controlled.
Modestly I want to live, modestly. Where the Herr
    Baron
Takes an Eiswein from the cellar, cradles it gently
In the tiny frozen hands of an echt Deutsch Mimi.
Where the quiet roebuck surround the hunting lodge,
Where the peasants, if they wanted, could shave with
    their hats.

Take me down to a Lustschloss in the year 1900,
Give me tea on the lawn of a vicarage garden,
Put me in a punt with all my little girl friends,
Let the dreams grow into the leafy sex-books.
I want a magnifying glass and a knowledge of Coptic
And a box in the British Museum for the last
    performance of Hamlet.

In and Out the Dusty Bluebells

'In and out the dusty bluebells'.
A children's game, a singing dance,
Rite of an urban Spring in wired-off playgrounds,
Clear voices dancing over traffic sounds.

'Tap-tap-tap on Someone's shoulder:'
With childishly expectant menace
The phrase stands up, and round it they all dance;
An antic frieze of children, they advance

Into a sinister future; where no rhymes
Hold up the threatening English sky,
Where clouds no bigger than a man's dark hand
Hold darker rain than they can understand.

Short Time

She juliets him from a window in Soho,
A 'business girl' of twenty.
He is a florid businessman of fifty.
(Their business is soon done.)

He, of a bright young man the sensual ghost,
Still (in his mind) the gay seducer,
Takes no account of thinned and greying hair,
The red veins webbing a once-noble nose,
The bushy eyebrows, wrinkles by the ears,
Bad breath, the thickening corpulence,
The faded, bloodshot eye.

This is his dream: that he is still attractive.

She, of a fashionable bosom proud,
A hairstyle changing as the fashions change,
Has still the ageless charm of being young,
Fancies herself and knows that men are mugs.

Her dream: that she has foxed the bloody world.

When two illusions meet, let there not be a third
Of the gentle hypocrite reader prone to think
That he is wiser than these self-deceivers.

Such dreams are common. Readers have them too.

The Middle Years

Between the pale young failure
And the bloated purple success
Lie the works on the life of the dahlia
Or the shrewd financial guess.

Between the love and the yearnings
And the fat indifference of age
Lie the greatly increased earnings
And the slick best-selling page.

Between the romantic lover
And the sordid dirty old man
Lies the fruitful wasted lifetime
Of the years that also ran.

A Christmas Message

In the few warm weeks
   before Christmas and the cold
the Toy Department is organized like a factory floor.
They're using epitaxial planar techniques
   in the labs. The toys are sold
and there's rationalized packaging and at the hot core

of the moving mass
   sweats a frost-powdered Father Christmas
in a red dressing-gown and an off-white beard.
What he wants most is a draught Bass.
   On a dry Hellenic isthmus
Zeus was a god who was equally hated and feared;

England is a Peloponnese
   and Father Christmas a poor old sod
like any other, autochthonous. Who believes
in the beard and the benevolence? Even in Greece
   or Rome there is only a bogus God
for children under five. Those he loves, he deceives.

Witchcraft

Last night you were being ridden by a governess,
A tall dark girl. Her transparent blouse
Showed the fat round nipples – all she wore.

She rocked on your pintle like a rocking-horse winner,
Squeezing so tight with elegant long thighs.
After five minutes, you began to change.

25

There were sulphurous fumes. Your sex curved inwards,
Your bosoms began to slowly plump and swell,
Your hair kaleidoscoped to new dispositions.

At last, in your plump thighs she triumphed,
With her new member and a hunting cry,
Whipping you towards the Sunday papers.

Crossing the Bar

My ambition is to live to be eighty,
To die quiet, surrounded by branded goods,
In perfect harmony like Oxo and Katie,
In a gamekeeper's cottage in the woods.

I want to drift towards my last Bournvita,
My children happy and a room of books
With their lined agony to make comfort sweeter,
Remembering the girls and their good looks.

I want all my employment to have been gainful,
My life to be free of angst and nuclear war,
And my last illness not to be terribly painful,
As I float in towards that distant shore.

Secrets of the Alcove

Quand' ero paggio . . .
I must have been adorable (I was certainly stupid).
The then Provost of King's
Chased me down two flights of stairs at a party.
Nearly twenty years later
A girl ran a hundred yards down a platform in Paris
In high-heeled shoes to kiss me.

All answered with a coldish heart.

Who has not had their little successes?
Inner absorption breaks into a rash of pride,
Shows in the visible signs of bad behaviour.
I regret my calmness in the face of love,
It bothers me like an unopened letter
Returned to sender, that now will never be read.

A Warning

A little fat genius is sitting there,
Small head, big belly.
A lot of brains under a little hair,
His sex organs – smelly.

That's the way it is with a genius,
He's always a bit odd.
He may have girl friends, grow zir
But he thinks he's a god.

Don't expect ordinary behaviour,
Or a guide to morals.
A genius is never a Saviour –
He only looks to his laurels.

War-time

A smooth bald head, a large white body.
No trace of pubic hair.
Raw, fretted and frayed by that rocky coast,
The flesh where the nipples were.

A woman drowned in war-time
On the Ligurian shore.
An Italian shouted *'E una femmina!'*
There seemed to be nothing more.

A suicide? A Resistance girl
From La Spezia floated down,
A murderee from Genoa?
The coast road into the town

Led me back to Livorno
And a British Army tea.
The war got hold of the women,
As it got hold of me.

Twenty years later, in the offices,
The typists tread out the wine,
Pounding with sharp stiletto heels,
Working a money mine.

It's a milder war, but it is one;
It's death by other means.
And I'm in the battle with them,
The soft recruits in their teens.

Office Friendships

Eve is madly in love with Hugh
And Hugh is keen on Jim.
Charles is in love with very few
And few are in love with him.

Myra sits typing notes of love
With romantic pianist's fingers.
Dick turns his eyes to the heavens above
Where Fran's divine perfume lingers.

Nicky is rolling eyes and tits
And flaunting her wiggly walk.
Everybody is thrilled to bits
By Clive's suggestive talk.

Sex suppressed will go berserk,
But it keeps us all alive.
It's a wonderful change from wives and work
And it ends at half past five.

Young

I'm a young giggle. Teenage. Sharp
Claws and an undulating tail,
Packaged in bright dreams of leather and teasing.
I like to make the boys excited
I love it when the cocks grow angry
My pulse jumps to the razor-fighting.

Their hands have run over me like mice
And I'm not mean, I let them have it.
Books like *The Woman* promise something different
But I can't spend my lifetime waiting.
The things you miss, you never get again.

My Mum and Dad know one word: Steady.
I'd rather mix it with a dozen boys,
Ice cream in different flavours. No one
Really wants vanilla all the time.

You split a coke, like on the telly,
And the two straws suck up your lifetime.
The sharing makes it quicker finished.

On your own you take the full flavour,
Get the longer, as-advertised pleasure.

I'll change when I change, but not before I do.

Variation on a Theme of A. Huxley

Some fat pigs are actually eating
And do not hesitate to name the parts:
Rumps, breasts and legs. It's revolting –
And done in the name of Science and the Arts.

They even describe the use of the instruments:
Knife, fork and spoon. It's bad for the Nation,
And can only lead to a terrible decadence
When they write a forbidden word like mastication.

See them revel in their beer and their beastliness,
Egged on by sherry, the bit between their teeth,
Ginned up for chambering and wantonness,
As round a hot frilled leg they garter a parsley wreath.

The Black Box

As well as these poor poems
I am writing some wonderful ones.
They are all being filed separately,
nobody sees them.

When I die they will be buried
in a big black tin box.
In fifty years' time
they must be dug up,

for so my will provides.
This is to confound the critics
and teach everybody
a valuable lesson.

June 1966

Lying flat in the bracken of Richmond Park
while the legs and voices of my children pass
seeking, seeking; I remember how on the
13th of June of that simmering 1940
I was conscripted into the East Surreys,
and, more than a quarter of a century
ago, when France had fallen,
we practised concealment in this very bracken.
The burnt stalks pricked through my denims.
Hitler is now one of the antiques of History,
I lurk like a monster in my hiding place.
He didn't get me. If there were a God
it would be only polite to thank him.

The Garden of the Clitorides

In the walled garden of the Clitorides
there's a paradise for middle-aged men
where the teenage girls come when they're called
and turn their eyes upwards in bitch-like adoration,
so perfect in their beauty of sleek prize-winning animals
it seems they never could die.

Perfect nakedness, perfect temperature, perfect idleness,
these are the dreams of middle-aged men.
Give or take some wines named by the gods.
Give or take some sleep in the perfumes of women.

Outside the garden lies a city of satire
peopled by parodies of garden behaviour –
the teasing stripshows, the expensive drunkenness,
the *noli me tangere* of vexatious virgins,
the falling into disrepute and destruction.

No one ever finds the gate to that garden.

Venus in Furs

There's a new opera called *I Masochisti*
With words by Freud and music by Bellini.
The first night's full of scented, furry women,
You can't have them. The conductor's baton
Puts an embargo on all base desires.
Under gold lamé the big nipples swell
Into crescendo. You're the muted horn
That sings of knighthood in the foyer bar.

Bullish, a stalled industrialist. He has it made.
His big bass voice comes straight up from his balls.
Whipped by desires, you're the derided one.
Nobody wants you, loves you, likes you.
Such marvellous deprivation! Can it last?

A Cup Too Low

Put on some Mozart. Then sit down and cry.
The world is very sad, and doesn't change.

Too many terrible people are people still.
It all looks bad, sounds bad; but don't be fooled,

It *is* bad. Though some of what you wanted
Perhaps you had. The wishes grow like weeds

Hemming you in till you can't see the sky
Or what is steadily flying out of range.

It's everything, not just the mind, that's ill.
Perhaps if all experience were pooled

The house of life would not be quite so haunted?
And happinesses grow from these sick seeds?

The Muse

A boy was kissing me left right and centre
But something nasty crept into his quatrains.
I left for thirty years. I haven't changed
Though he's grey at the edges. Now I'm back
We live together in uneasy joy.

My lovely mouth; his bitter, tainted kiss
On sufferance like an old and worn-out husband.
The boys are waving in the other bar,
I swing my skirts and go. A long goodbye
To all who woo me when they're past their prime.

Beginnings

In the vast antheap of the world
one little ant thinks differently.

In the snarled traffic of metropolis
a small family car crashes the lights.

Under a tailored and conventional suit
a heart beats out a naked rhythm.

Like a roomsize coloured balloon
a man blows up a religion till it bursts.

Somebody somewhere begins to unpick the stitches
in the bright battle flag of glory.

Daddyo

My hearing deadens. My eyes
aren't good in artificial light.
The memory wobbles. But
that's enough of that.

So clearly I remember
what a harsh crass old man
my father seemed
thirty years ago.

But he was the bright boy
from Edinburgh, the medico who won
hundreds of pounds of weighty scholarships.
A big attacking surgeon.

My mind shrank under the barking knife.

Now it's my turn
to be the red-faced fool
that sons hate, tittered at
by sneering miniskirts.

It's strange to wear
a dead man's shoes, to know
exactly where
each one pinches.

Arithmetic

I'm 11. And I don't really know
my Two Times Table. Teacher says it's disgraceful
But even if I had the time, I feel too tired.
Ron's 5, Samantha's 3, Carole's 18 months,
and then there's Baby. I do what's required.

Mum's working. Dad's away. And so
I dress them, give them breakfast. Mrs Russell
moves in, and I take Ron to school.
Miss Eames calls me an old-fashioned word: Dunce.
Doreen Maloney says I'm a fool.

After tea, to the Rec. Pram-pushing's slow
but on fine days it's a good place, full
of larky boys. When 6 shows on the clock
I put the kids to bed. I'm free for once.
At about 7 – Mum's key in the lock.

A Woman's World

I'm being raped by an apeman
when the egg-timer pings in the kitchen,
the excited kettle comes in steam.

My lover has blue scales instead of skin,
I grind against him like cheese under a grater.
There are birds seven feet high,
I ride them down the motorways.
All gooey with blood; and fighting.
I am an Empress, pop from the beds
of the warm soldiers like toast from the machine.

It's red-hot buggery for the cheeky secretaries
my husband plays with.

One for the Anthologies

Herbert's a hard and horrid man
    And so am I.
He does as much harm as he can
    And so do I.
He wastes the time of Institutes
And spends his nights with prostitutes,
    And so do I.

Wilfred's a weak and weary man
    And so am I.
He's always been an also-ran
    And so have I.
He's been defeated all his life,
Too tired to end it with a knife –
    And so am I.

David's a dense and drunken man
    And so am I.
He's fond of glass and mug and can
    And so am I.
When these sad dogs have had their day
They'll all be glad to go away
    And so will I.

Xmas for the Boys

A clockwork skating Wordsworth on the ice,
An automatic sermonizing Donne,
A brawling Marlowe shaking out the dice,
A male but metaphysical Thom Gunn.
Get them all now – the latest greatest set
Of all the Poets, dry to sopping wet.

A mad, ferocious, disappointed Swift
Being beaten by a servant in the dark.
Eliot going up to Heaven in a lift,
Shelley going overboard, just for a lark.
Although the tempo and the talent varies
Now is the time to order the whole series.

An electronic Milton, blind as a bat,
A blood-spitting consumptive Keats,
Tennyson calmly raising a tall hat,
Swinburne being whipped in certain dark back streets.
All working models, correct from head to toe –
But Shakespeare's extra, as you ought to know.

Ella Mi Fu Rapita!

'Die Liebe dauert oder dauert nicht'
BRECHT

Her boredom took her away. So simple.
She just became bored with me. No other rival
experienced the entrancing smile with the dimple
or put down his drink in joy at her arrival
or loved her in taxis that stream like ants
through London, fingers under her pants

caressing her holy of holies. Oh, no
it wasn't someone younger, bigger or better.
She went because she had the urge to go,
without a phone call, telegram or letter.
From our last meeting she just walked out –
a few pretexts perhaps. What were they about?

Nothing too serious. A red bow in her hair,
as she lay naked on the bed, knees-raising,
stays in my mind. I know I had my share.
Love is all programmed, it's all phasing,
there's a beginning, a middle and an end.
A lover's life is not that of a friend,

who by and large is able to take it or leave it.
For love there's a critical path – it goes on.
It can't go backwards or sideways, believe it,
that's all; a dream, a tremendous con,
and when it's over, you're out on your own.
Most life, they say, has to be lived alone.

And what can the lover do, when the time's come,
when THE END goes up on the screen? Yelling,
rush into the street, lamenting her lovely bum?
Get friendly with men in bars, telling
how sweet she was, praising her statistics,
or admiring his own sexual ballistics?

No, that's no good. Love lasts – or doesn't last.
And all the pink intimacies and warm kisses
go into Proust's remembrance of time past.
Lovers must never crumple up like cissies
or break down or cry about their wrongs.
If girls are sugar, God holds the sugar tongs.

The Pseudo-Demetrius *

After the summer on the lovely island
came the pretender, the autumn of the city,
the Pseudo-Demetrius garlanded with blackberries;
the true young one had strawberries and raspberries
and the real love in the matchless bed.

After the moistness of the pink lips opening
came the equivocal, the Pseudo-Demetrius,
the one who told us he would make us equal
to what we were when the flowers were young ones
and we knew love in the matchless bed.

After the sun's hour, the failing succession
came with a turbulence but no tenderness,
the anger and envy of the Pseudo-Demetrius,
the one who stirred up trouble and caused the ending
of our best love in the matchless bed.

After the green and the bees in clover
came the new season when we were forgotten,
the riot and sadness of the Pseudo-Demetrius,
brown leaves falling on the musclemen fighting,
and no real love in the matchless bed.

After the summer, after the sun's hour,
came the equivocal, turbulent pretender,
the Pseudo-Demetrius garlanded with autumn,
with lies and fighting in the darkened city,
and death, not love, in the matchless bed.

* In the history of medieval Russia there are two Pretenders.
They are called Pseudo-Demetrius I and Pseudo-Demetrius II.

Victorian

Miss with the vapours.
The claret and the oysters.
The curling papers.
Fat clergy in the cloisters.

Heavy squires hunting.
Pints of port and porter.
Grumbling and grunting.
Gothic bricks and mortar.

Fog in the dockyards.
Decorum at the Palace.
Blood in the stockyards.
Murder in the alleys.

The Select Party

Hands that wiped arses
are holding glasses,
lips that fellated
are intoxicated,
parts that were randy
have counterparts handy –

but the fact of a quorum
preserves decorum,
and the social unction
inhibits the function
of the natural passions
concealed by the fashions.

Tongues that licked scrota
don't move one iota

from the usual phrases
that the century praises,
the undisturbed labia
are deserted Arabia –

these cats are all mousers
but skirts and trousers
keep the lid on the kettle;
there are magnets, there's metal,
but they don't click together
thru nylon and leather.

The Sentimental Education

Wear your Thomas Hardy suit and sit with candles in the
   gloom.
Summon ghosts of years departed till they fill the empty
   room.

First of all call up the weather – heatwave 1922,
Wartime winters with the blackout, blossom on the trees
   at Kew.

Then the people. First, a nanny. Next, your father
   wearing spats.
Mummy with her pearls at evening, and her three
   amazing cats.

Childish captions fit the pictures – you were very childish
   then –
But you see it still as clearly as the present world of men.

Peter Pan was pulsing drama, green lights shone on
   Captain Hook.
Carroll's Jabberwock caused nightmares, till you had to
   hide the book.

You were one. Then came two sisters. They were
    different from you.
You liked best fried bread and cocoa, loved the zebras at
    the Zoo.

Then the schools – a bourgeois saga – we all know what
    they were like.
Minnows in a pond, a bully swam among them like a
    pike.

Squeeze them in? You'd need a ballroom. Still
    remembered, many names
Cluster round in shorts and sweaters. Latin, algebra and
    games.

Chapel services. Then freedom, and the length of King's
    Parade.
Dadie, Anthony – and Classics, all the dons that had it
    made.

Cicero made ghastly speeches, elegiacs were a bore.
You had two years in the saltmines – how could you
    come up for more?

Next was English, Richards lectures, Leavis supervising.
    Fine.
English literature went down as stimulating as new wine.

After Cambridge – unemployment. No one wanted
    much to know.
Good degrees are good for nothing in the business world
    below.

In the end you were a salesman, selling lithographic
    prints.
Trade was stagnant after Munich. Hitler frightened us
    with hints.

War came down, a blackout curtain, shutting out the
    kindly sun.
Jews went under, all the playboys somehow lost their
    sense of fun.

Still, we always had the weather – freezing cold or hot as
hell –
Birds continued, flowers were rampant, life went on
through shot and shell.

Back at last to shabby London, tired and rationed, sad to
see,
With its tales of air raid wardens, siren suits and hot sweet
tea.

People, literary people, now replaced the roaring boys
Fond of vino, signorinas, dirty jokes and lots of noise.

Tambi, Nicholas and Helen. Come on in. You see them
plain.
Publishing will never, surely, be as odd as that again.

Money, said the British Council, I have money in my
hand.
Get your hair cut, keep your nose clean, live in Civil
Serviceland.

Six years later came the end game – middle grades were
axed. Goodbye!
They were victims of the Beaver's petulant persistent
cry.

Advertising. Advertising. Fatal Lady of the Lake!
No one opts for copywriting, they get in there by
mistake.

You absorbed those business ethics – not the Sermon on
the Mount –
Walked into that artful parlour, had the William Hill
account.

Let the room explode with whizz kids, dollies, every
kind of Pop!
Only crematorium silence brings that mayhem to a stop.

Money. Children. Mortgage. Rat race. Anxious words
that tax the brain.
Nagging fears of unemployment drive the middle class
insane.

It's not pretty when they throw you, screaming, in the
empty sack,
Filled with nothing but the cries of wives and children
screaming back.

Does the working class get ulcers? No one worries much,
if so.
They know jobs are hard to come by, and the pay is often
low.

They're inured to thoughts of hardship and of being out
of work.
This is life. It's no good blubbing, throwing fits or going
berserk.

Moneyed men in Lloyds, the City, can't imagine what
it's like.
To the driver of an E-type, what's the old penurious
bike?

Workmen are a bloody nuisance – just a ROAD UP sign
or two –
Obstacles that spoil their record from the Bank to Luton
Hoo.

Keep your voice down. Don't start shouting. Let the
candles burn up straight.
(Privileged and trendy diners stuff themselves with After
Eight.)

All you learn – and from a lifetime – is that that's the way
it goes.
That's the crumbling of the cookie, till the turning up of
toes.

2001: The Tennyson/Hardy Poem

When I am old and long turned grey
And enjoy the aura of being eighty,
I may see the dawn of that critical day
When my lightest verse will seem quite weighty.
I shall live somewhere far away,
Where the illiterate birds are nesting.
To pilgrim admirers my wife will say:
          Ewart is resting.

Instead of the heedless sensual play
And the youthful eyes of love and brightness
I shall see critics who kneel and pray
In homage – I shan't dispute their rightness –
And Supplements keen to seem okay
Will flatter me with fulsome pieces.
Scholars will put it another way:
          Ewart's a thesis.

When the aching back and the bleary eye
And the dimness and the rationed drinking,
The cold unease of the earth and sky,
Leave me no pleasures except thinking
I shall be warmed (but what will be 'I'?)
With the awe inspired by what's Jurassic,
And people will say, before I die:
          Ewart's a classic.

Soon comes the day when the stream runs dry
And the boat runs back as the tide is turning,
The voice once strong no more than a sigh
By the hearth where the fire is scarcely burning.
Stiff in my chair like a children's guy,
Simply because I have no seniors
The literati will raise the cry:
          Ewart's a genius!

Sonnet: The Last Things

Of course there's always a last everything.
The last meal, the last drink, the last sex.
The last meeting with a friend. The last
stroking of the last cat, the last
sight of a son or daughter. Some would be more
charged with emotion than others – if one knew.
It's not knowing that makes it all so piquant.
A good many lasts have taken place already.

Then there are last words, variously reported,
such as: Let not poor Nelly starve. Or:
I think I could eat one of Bellamy's veal pies.
If there were time I'd incline to a summary:
Alcohol made my life shorter but more interesting.
My father said (not last perhaps): Say goodbye to Gavin.

To a Plum-Coloured Bra Displayed in Marks & Spencer

The last time I saw you, as like as two pins,
you were softly supporting those heavenly twins
that my hands liberated before the gas fire
in the mounting impatience of driving desire,

when the nipples appeared with their cherry-ripe tips,
so inviting to fingers and tongues and to lips
as they hardened and pardoned my roughness and haste
and both had, like her body, a feminine taste.

You're a bra made in millions, promiscuously sold –
but your sister contained something dearer than gold.
Mass-production, seduction; you've got it all there
on that counterfeit torso so cold and so bare,

but you serve to remind me, as nothing else could,
of the heartbeats and touching, what's tender and good.
I could ikon you, candle you, kneel on the floor,
my love's symbol of richness – in all else I'm poor!

Hurried Love

Those who make hurried love don't do so
from any lack of affection
or because they despise their partner
as a human being –
what they're doing
is just as sincere as a more formal wooing.

She may have a train to catch; perhaps the
room is theirs for one hour only
or a mother is expected back or
some interruption
known, awaited –
so the spur of the moment must be celebrated.

Making love against time is really
the occupation of all lovers
and the clock-hands moving
point a moral:
not crude, but clever
are those who grab what soon is gone for ever.

Memory Man

I'm sitting drinking Guinness
in memory of you,
on the wall is written Finis
and although the love was true –
if I were more romantic I would say sublime –
it was not a love that lasted until closing time.

The glasses are being polished
as they shout 'Last orders, please!'
and illusions are demolished
with the same fantastic ease
as the ease with which Joe closes his democratic bar –
if I think of you now, it's 'you were' and not 'you are'.

Each man that loves a woman
must be prepared for this
for a sexual love is human
and betrayal by a kiss
is a commonplace and not just in the holy Book
and it all begins when your eyes take that first long look.

You must have the boldness
to overcome the moods,
the sulking and the coldness,
your love must feed on foods
which wouldn't keep alive a common tabby cat;
no one can have *this* without an awful lot of *that*.

So it's sadly time to drink up
and let them stack the chairs –
he's a wise man who can think up
a remedy that bears
much resemblance to an answer (Venus is a jerk?);
for that holiday is over – from now on it's back to work.

The Larkin Automatic Car Wash

Back from the Palace of a famous king,
  Italian art
Making the roped-off rooms a Culture thing,
At about five o'clock we made a start,
Six teenagers squashed in. And as I drove
North from the barley sugar chimney pots
They sang the changeable teenager songs
That fade like tapestries those craftsmen wove,
But centuries more quickly. Through the knots
Of road-crossing pedestrians, through the longs

And shorts of planners' morse, the traffic lights,
  Over a hill,
Down to the garage advertising tights,
A special bargain, fast I drove on till
I drew up by the new Car Wash machine,
Pride of the forecourt, where a sign said STOP
Clear on the asphalt. In front a smaller car
Stood patiently as brushes swooshed it clean,
Whirling its streaming sides and back and top –
A travelling gantry; verticals, cross-bar.

We wound our windows up and waited there.
  In pixie green
The moving monster lifted itself clear,
The yellow brushes furled and now were seen
As plastic Christmas trees. Its wet last client
Made for the highway and it was our turn.
In gear and under. Two tenpences fed in
A slot on the driver's side. The pliant
Great brushes whirred and closed. Like yellow fern
One blurred the windscreen. Underwater thin

The Science Fiction light came creeping through
  Alien and weird
As when the vegetables invade in *Dr Who*,
Something to be amused at – almost feared.

And as the lateral brushes closed our sides,
Sweeping past steadily back, the illusion came
That *we* were moving forward; and I checked
The hard-on handbrake, thought of switchback rides
And how the effect in childhood was the same –
Momentary fear that gathered, to collect

In joy of safety. The tall half-children screamed –
    The girls at least –
Delighted to be frightened, as it seemed,
By this mechanical, otherworldly beast.
The boys made usual, window-opening, jokes.
And soon, tide-turning, the brushes travelled back,
Put our imaginations in reverse,
Though we were still. Like cigarettes and cokes
This was their slight excitement, took up slack
In time that wound by, idle. Nothing worse

And nothing better. To me it seemed so short,
    I wanted more,
I wanted hours, I wanted to be caught
In that dense undergrowth by that wet shore.
This was an exit from our boring life,
A changed environment, another place,
A hideout from the searchers. Otherness
Was that world's commonplace, a kitchen knife,
Something so usual that it had no face –
As the car dripped unnatural cleanliness.

Yes, it was jolly, *Fun for the kids* we say,
    But more than that;
For if you look at it another way
This was a notable peak where all is flat.
Into the main road by the riverside
We right-turned past the pubs that line the route
Where cheering crowds watch boat race crews go by,
Travelling with the full incoming tide.
The roof, the sides, the bonnet and the boot
Shone with new wetness. Yet the dust could lie

As thick there as before; and would, in time,
   This was reprieve.
Cars too grow old and dirty. Gin-and-lime
Perks up the guest; but all guests have to leave.
In through the main gate of the block of flats
I drove my giggling adolescent load,
And in vibrating door-slammed solitude
I parked. Under their different hats
Spiritual experiences work in a kind of code.
Did I have one? I, from this multitude?

Trafalgar Day, 1972

All bathed and brindled like a brushed cat,
with a slight hangover from a literary party
(and what could be nicer than that?)

on the day that one-armed bandit finally bought it
I celebrate your sixteenth birthday;
Who (one could say) would have thought it,

when I was a neurotic sixteen at Wellington College,
that I should ever be a girl's *father*,
straining after poetry and carnal knowledge?

But there you are and here I am, and let it be believed
it was during a broadcast performance
of Mozart's *Idomeneo* that you were conceived.

So the whirligig of time brings in his revenges
(don't quote me on that one)
and something as mystical as our lost Stonehenges

has added another link to the chain of being,
making you real and believable,
and believing is (believe me) rather like seeing,

as you get stuck into *Jude the Obscure*,
in the gear of your generation;
Hardy certainly thought that Tess was pure

and said so on the title page. Though this is a concept
and a word that doesn't apply
much nowadays, and words themselves are inept

to transmit a person's quality, you've got a womanly
    feeling
of the kind men often lack.
That's what makes women, mainly, so appealing,

and when the hawks gather round to bully a dove
you'd be soft-hearted; and
the emotion you inspire in me could, loosely, be called
    love.

Consoler Toujours

All bright love that strikes like lightning on our so-so lives
            is a bonus,
like the honey bees are making in their secret hives
            and the onus
to enjoy it is on us as decrepitude arrives,
            each Tithonus

remembering the years-ago girls clearly in his heart,
          not forgetting
all those faces and those kisses, every sexual part,
          heavy petting,
and each happy ending from a slow or frantic start,
          and its setting

—all those rooms that now hold others or are bulldozed down,
          flats and houses
standing tall as ghosts and ghostly in a ghostly town.
          The mind drowses
quietly on the beds and sofas, red, white, pink or brown.
          This arouses

old emotions, recollected in tranquillity.
          Thought's assizes
try the case of W or beauties B and C,
          no disguises
hide the naked A; as she is sleeping there so peacefully
          the sun rises. . .

Women count and hoard their lovers for the days ahead,
          single-bedding,
long last hours in hospitals, know towards what bed
          they are heading
and what bells will ring for them at that lonely dead
          last wedding;

theirs and ours, the lovely bodies end up in a mess
          or disgusting.
Yet these are the hands that fumbled to undo a dress,
          young and trusting
we gave sexual adoration, love and tenderness,
          June was busting

out all over like a song (and that's a fairly old
          jazz song title)
so let's remember that we had it – something gleamed like gold,
          very vital,
something beautiful and better than time's creeping cold
          sad requital.

Sonnet: Cat Logic

Cat sentimentality is a human thing. Cats
are indifferent, their minds can't comprehend
the concept 'I shall die', they just go on living.
Death is more foreign to their thought than
to us the idea of a lime-green lobster. That's
why holding these warm containers of purring fur
is poignant, that they just don't *know*.
Life is in them, like the brandy in the bottle.

One morning a cat wakes up, and doesn't feel
disposed to eat or wash or walk. It doesn't panic
or scream: 'My last hour has come!' It
simply fades. Cats never go grey at the edges
like us, they don't even look old. Peter Pans,
insouciant. No wonder people identify with cats.

The Hut

That is the hut where she used to work; and there
        under the paint-peeled corrugated iron
with square small windows set in wooden frames
by thumb and spatula she played the old Art games;
        under the moon now, far from bright Orion,
in misty autumn, tenantless and bare

it stands so useless in the bleakly chilling air,
        nettle-surrounded, a falling garden shed,
and cobwebbed to the mean and spidered roof,
sad as great Abbeys – for Time is so aloof,
        indifferent to that life that once she led
when she sat smoking in that single chair.

The canvases have gone. Some empty frames odd-piled,
    African figures on the windowsill,
witness the young Slade student of shared youth,
paint-splashes hold a bitter kind of truth,
    the easel stands at ease in empty drill.
And with these things I must be reconciled.

The friends and sisters go; and all who had in that past smiled
    (and some had beauty, some were bright with wit)
must forfeit health and come to this one room
as dark with memory as a Victorian tomb,
    and we must wrestle with understanding it
until from life and hope we are exiled.

Venus

A goddess has just checked out and
left no forwarding address. She won't be back.
She got so bored with waiting. For so many years
you spoke of her slightingly.
Telephone calls. The unshared drinks at six.
She took in movies, slept late. Oh, yes
she knew you, expected you.

If she was lying in a bath relaxing
and fingering the soap as goddesses do
she was certainly working out an alias.
We only know them under other names.
They change. As the light falls on a building,
changing it. Perhaps she even
had a name for *you*?

Long lunches, scented bedrooms, cold trays
with hot coffee and perhaps an egg.
She had the life of an émigrée, the small
dictatorial smile for room service,
kept clean, kept beautiful.
But now she's gone. You won't see her
again or ever. It's an empty room.

The Theory of the Leisure Class

In those huge Victorian novels that were written during
    the time when Tennyson was occupied with Marianas
    and Mauds
people were saying things like 'What do you think, my
    dear sir, in general, of pious frauds?'
and the language was pompous in the extreme and you
    might guess they one and all were as cold-blooded as
    saurians;
though we know now they all had Secret Lives and were
    having a high old time with those Other Victorians.

There were *malades imaginaires* and interesting invalids
    and ladies with permanently weakened constitutions,
while the rough gin-drinking populace starved or
    enjoyed themselves at public executions.
The ambition of the wealthy was, quite seriously, to do
    absolutely nothing but to drink, to ride, to dance, to
    flirt.
Gambling for high stakes, soldiering, politics, the
    buying of a new horse or a new skirt.

These were the only approved interests. Making money
    was trade. It must have been very gentlemanly but
    boring,
especially for the ladies, who weren't allowed – like their
    husbands and boy friends – to go off whoring.

Governesses suffered most. They had to be well-behaved
    examples and quite preternaturally respectable.
They couldn't get drunk or encourage (or satisfy the
    desires of) men, however delectable.

In a hundred years or so we've changed, with our
    haircuts and our democratic adolescents in classless
    clothes,
though those with the wealth don't show many signs of
    being terribly different from those
whose motto (What We Have We Hold) they held – as Mr
    Mantalini might say – 'like some demd vempire',
and our commercial predominance hasn't survived
    two wars and the disposal of an Empire.

Almost every class now is a leisure class, occupied (as it
    might be) with The Who, The Beatles or Bingo,
turned on by the telly, passively entertained by electronic
    football, Ken Russell, Ringo.
It all makes one think of bread and circuses, of those
    century-gone lives idle and under a blight;
how William Morris, who wanted handicrafts instead of
    machines, might very well have been right.

Incident, Second World War

(In Memoriam P. M. B. Matson)

It was near the beginning of that war. 1940 or '41,
when everything was fairly new to almost everyone.
The bombing of cities we understood, and blackouts;
    and certainly, thanks
to the German Army and Air Force, we'd seen
    dive-bombers and tanks.

But when the fighters came in to strafe with
   hedge-hopping low attacks
how many bits and pieces would be picked up to fill the
   sacks?
Aircraft cannon were not much fun for the weary
   grounded troops
and there wasn't much entertainment when the Stukas
   were looping loops
but nobody knew for certain the percentage who
   wouldn't get up,
how many would be donating their arms or their legs to
   Krupp.
So somebody in an office had the very bright idea,
why not set up an Exercise: machine-gunning from the
   air?
The War Office would know exactly the kind of figures
   involved,
an exciting statistical problem could be regarded as
   solved.

In a field, they put khaki dummies, on the reverse side of
   a hill.
And afterwards, they reckoned, they could estimate the
   kill.
Opposite these was the audience, to watch the total
   effect,
a sort of firework display – but free – the R A F being the
   architect.
All arms were represented? I think so. A grandstand seat
was reserved for top brass and others, a healthy open-air
   treat;
enclosed, beyond the dummies, they stood (or sat?) and
   smoked
or otherwise passed the time of day, relaxed as they
   talked and joked.

An experienced Spitfire pilot was briefed to fly over low
and give those dummies all he'd got – the star turn of the
   show,

with all the verisimilitude of a surprise attack.
Then to his fighter station he would whizz round and
     back.
They waited. And suddenly, waiting, they saw that
     angel of death
come at them over the hillside. Before they could draw
     breath
he passed with all guns firing; some fell on their faces,
     flat,
but the benefit was minimal that anyone had from that.
He reckoned that *they* were the dummies, in his
     slap-happy lone-wolf way,
that trigger-crazy pilot. He might have been right, some
     say.
But bitterness and flippancy don't compensate for men's
     lives
and official notifications posted to mothers and wives.

Nevertheless, there *were* results; percentages were
     worked out,
how 10 per cent could be written off, the wounded
     would be about
50 per cent or so. Oh yes, they got their figures all right.
Circulated to units. So at least that ill-omened flight
was a part of the Allied war effort, and on the credit side —
except for those poor buggers who just stood there and
     died.

Yeats and Shakespeare

Somebody wrote somewhere (about Yeats)
how even in those wasp-waisted days
before the First World War
(for twenty years reckoned among the Greats)
he was so spoiled by worship and by praise
he couldn't behave naturally any more,

That hand, once in mine, was in his as you walked
    And answered him in your bright treble;
Not a word could I hear but I knew that you talked
    And the Flesh rose up like a dark rebel –
For that hand, as I knew, was an adjunct to Love,
    Like a hot caper sauce to hot mutton,
And designed by the Lord to descend from above
    First to fondle – and then to unbutton!

Ah! those feet that ran to me won't run to me now,
    The dismal and desperate fact is
They will turn to avoid me, for you will know how
    To go home with the Choir after Practice –
Though you lingered once sweetly to dally with me
    And our preoccupations weren't choral
As you sat in the sitting-room there on my knee
    And the examination was oral!

I saw those eyes opening, gazing at him
    With the blue of the midsummer heaven,
My own eyes with traitorous tear-drops grew dim
    And of Rage, lustful Rage, a black leaven
Worked in me there; for those eyes once had seen
    (Thought to break my heart, break it and rive it)
On the ottoman, proud in its velvety green,
    Those parts that our God has called private!

I dream of a Paradise still, now and then,
    But it is not the orthodox milieu
Where good spirits abound – with no women or men.
    Ah! My Conscience lies drowned like Ophelia!
And my Heaven's a dream of an opulent South
    With soft cushions, wine, perfumes, bells ringing,
My member for ever held tight in your mouth
    And a thousand bright choirboys all singing!

To Lord Byron

on the occasion of the 150th anniversary of his death,
commemorated at the Victoria and Albert Museum

You didn't much like relics. The 'lying bust'
    seemed to you too impersonal and cold
to represent warm flesh, whose love and lust
    even the Puritans share (when not too old)
before they crumble into decent dust.
    What would *you* think of this? Would you feel 'sold'?
For geniuses, alas, it's a tradition
to end up as a paying Exhibition.

So here are portraits of that gang you banged,
    the bright, unstable, intellectual ladies;
evidence that an ancestor was nearly hanged
    (to roam, unblessed, the further shores of Hades),
that in the Lords you once stood and harangued
    and kept a bear at Cambridge. A bill (paid?) is
exhibited as proof (bear food and lodging) –
though, through your life, your debts were not for dodging.

Here, from Miss Chaworth to La Guiccioli,
    with delicate miniatures and locks of hair,
are philosophical ladies, prophetic, Nietzschely,
    high-waisted with their bosoms raised and bare –
but also bakers' wives, untamed, unteacherly,
    one that was married to a gondolier.
That auburn curl (for some peculiar reason)
of Lady Caroline Lamb gave me a *frisson*.

Pathetic, too, to read Allegra's letters
    in copybook Italian, guided by nuns,
who went to join her elders and her betters
    under those feverish Mediterranean suns

at five years old. *Caro Papa*. Hounds, setters,
　　horses you kept. Children were shunned like duns.
Shelley, a guest at your Venetian palace,
was right to be angry and to call you callous.

But who am I to take a stance that's moral?
　　Your entourage was not for little girls.
In any case it's far too late to quarrel –
　　you were worth fifty of *our* Lords and Earls,
in days when atom bombs shake ocean coral
　　we are the swine to whom you cast your pearls,
you stand like some far-shining distant lighthouse.
And what would you have thought of Mrs Whitehouse?

Would you be keen on Peter Pan and Wendy
　　or anything that's cosy, coy or twee?
Contrariwise, would you admire what's trendy
　　(you were a fashion once yourself) or see
virtue in what's suburban or weekendy?
　　To you, who only knew one kind of tea,
who never knew what roaches or a jag meant,
I dedicate this small Byronic fragment.

The Gentle Sex (1974)

　　　　On Tuesday, 23 July,
　　　　in that black sectarian Belfast
　　under a rainy, cramped and hopeless sky
　　　　five Loyalist women at last,
　　after a false alarm visit the previous day,
　　found Anne Ogilby in her home; under overcast
　　　　weather, in a little car, they drove her away,
leaving behind her five-year-old daughter Sharlene, who
　　could only scream and cry.

67

Leader of the Women's UDA,
   Lilly Douglas was in charge.
For questioning, to hear what Anne had to say
   (for cloudy suspicions were looming large
over the little terraced houses of Sandy Row,
full of memories of unemployment and bread and
   marge)
   why food-parcel money, that by rights should go
on food for her boy friend in Long Kesh, had gone (they
claimed) astray.

Each month £10.
   One of the women accusing,
who hunted her down, we could say, like hounds,
   found it far from amusing
that her husband was the boy friend who had lived
   with Anne
for a full three months before arrest, refusing
   to return home, father of Anne's baby, a man
who had had enough of her and her marital life – that's
how it sounds.

They drove to a Loyalist club
   and questioned her, hard and mean;
but then a UDA man from a pub
   happened to intervene –
this was lucky for her indeed, and it certainly fell
out luckily that he should have come on the scene.
   At a bus station by the Europa Hotel
they left her, released; as scared cats leave birds and dive
under a shrub.

A dark 31-year-old,
   unmarried mother of four;
and even a British soldier, the women told,
   was father of one, a whore
they couldn't call her, pots don't call kettles black,

but they also said, and protested, a very great deal
        more
    about betrayed gunmen; a Protestant murder attack
she had witnessed, and the 'kneecapping' of a sheep that
    tried to leave the fold.

        Just after 10.15
        Lilly Douglas's teenage daughter
    and another girl, only sixteen,
        stood in front of her bus and caught her.
    They dragged her off. In a small red Fiat, nine
    women started off to a 'Romper Room' in that quarter
        where their traitors are disciplined – fine
for the beaters-up but for the others the fun isn't so good
    and clean.

        But, before they arrived, the car
        was stopped by police, who took
        them all back to the bus station; so far
        no crime – so whom could they book?
    Anne, the police say, kept nervously biting her nails
    but refused to make a complaint (though she did look
        like someone in need of help). Law fails
always where the community knows, and won't tell,
    who the killers are.

        At 10.30, then, next day
        (home in the small hours) she
        failed to attend at the Welfare; but they
        know she was there at three.
    Meanwhile, in the Elm Bar, a 'heavy squad' was
        drinking –
    'Bumper' Graham, three unemployed teenage girls. The
    key
        to the whole situation, the woman of action and
        thinking
was 41-year-old Lilly, smuggler, forger, violent, drunk,
    brothel-keeper (police say).

Convicted, too. Gave order:
Graham to fetch Anne from Welfare.
He went. Without force, no lawless marauder,
found her and took her from there.
The welfare officers had not even, then, been seen.
In an Edinburgh hostel, safe in their care,
a place had been found, for both Anne and Sharlene.
This she never knew. Of such missed trains and wrong
destinations Time's a relentless hoarder.

But now: the Romper Room. And,
when Sharlene began to cry,
Graham put 10p into her childish hand,
said she'd see Mammy bye and bye
and told her to go out and buy herself some sweets.
Her mother was blindfolded with a tea towel; we
know why
a dark brown bag was put over her head. In the
streets
meanwhile life flowed easy in the uneasy city, like the sea
lapping the sand.

Etty Cowan, Chrissie Smith, Joey Brown
wearing, all three, white masks
made from one of Joey's jumpers (put down,
it sounds like a game; but such tasks
come easy in the boredom and poverty of their
existence),
walked in and began to 'romper' Anne. Who asks,
in such circumstances, exactly why? No resistance
was offered as she was pushed and kicked from one to the
other – like a circus clown.

Graham and Joey were upset
by now. They tried to stop it.
But Etty Cowan was in her stride, all set,
took a brick and wouldn't drop it,

stood over Anne and banged it on her face,
as hard as she could, a very determined moppet.
    She and Chrissie stopped for a smoke. Some
        minutes' grace
she had from that; but soon they began again, giving it all
    they'd got – or could get.

        Outside the door Sharlene,
            back with a chocolate biscuit, screamed
        (inside, her mother screamed; obscene
            thumps, thuds, gurgles seemed
    the soundtrack of a nightmare, 'Mammy, I want my
        Mammy!'
    echoed outside, a bad dream crudely dreamed),
        through the brown bag perhaps the blood oozed,
            jammy –
until she twitched no longer; even for those avengers, the
    slate wiped clean.

        So when they knew that she'd died
            they went for a bottle of wine.
        They just shooed Sharlene outside
            and onto the streets. The deep mine
    of vengeance was plumbed, the boil lanced.
    The body? Disposed on a motorway. Fine.
        They got into a disco and danced.
For a good cause, and a mother's jealousy revenged, can
    make you feel warm inside.

        Oedema of the brain,
            associated fractures of the skull,
        and on the scalp the deepened main
            sixteen separate wounds. Dull
    their lives must have been, dull and dull indeed
    for this to be their pleasure! The wayward gull
        floats over Belfast; animals have no need
for torture. Her face was completely black. And
    certainly, chewing gum in court, they'd do it again.

'The Lion griefs loped from the shade
And on our knees their muzzles laid,
    And Death put down his book'

                    Don't worry,
poetry won't be as good as that again in a hurry!
                New 'schools', now,
may regard us as a collection of old fools now,
                    or wonder
what on earth we saw in it – but, no blunder,
                what Bach had
(strict formal beauty), what *The Hunting of the Snark* had,
                    corroding
and surreal anxiety, a sense of foreboding,
                    and, in it
all too, the urgency of the actual historical minute –
                these made it
more compelling than the craftsman's ear by which he
    played it.

                    Each age, I
submit, has its own particular Journey of the Magi;
                they carry
the gifts that alone can truly, faithfully, marry
                    the ideal
to our hesitating, wavering sense of what is real.
                    So Auden
threw round the political nasties a sort of cordon,
                    immunizing
us against their infecting presence, and rising,
                    a champion,
a serious singer, a warner, a Baptist, a Campion
                    with social
significance (a prophet whose 'Woe!' shall
                be ignored – as
it always is – no more regarded than Harry Lauder's
                brash singing)
came at us like Carroll's Bellman with that bell he was
    ringing!

72

                    Swinburne too
once with the young men at Oxford certainly had his
     turn – to
                    be chanted
in evening streets. For some sort of Saviour is wanted.
                    Dogmatics
are twenty years old, with bats in their belfries and attics,
                    a top storey
that leans, not to work or moderation, but to death and
     glory,
                    new magic –
Auden's wonderful hybrid rose that crossed the comic
     with the tragic.

Perchance a Jealous Foe

It was Spring when Annabel came to Stoatswold.
The old house lay slumbering in the warm Spring
     sunshine
as though waiting for something to happen. Nothing
     happened.
The smoke just curled up lazily from Elizabethan
     chimneys
as it had for generations of incumbent Stoatswolds,
an old family and proud of it – from before the Normans.
(In fact, the present owner was Sir Norman Stoatswold,
a widower who smoked a pipe in the Long Garden
and was well–known locally for the quality of his
     shorthorns).

73

Annabel came, of course, as a governess. Her young charge
was pretty little Myfanwy Stoatswold, fifteen and headstrong.
She was called Myfanwy because her dead mother
had been a Welsh Nationalist (and hated Suffolk).
Annabel often wondered if she would have been called Fiona
if the nationality had been otherwise. She never asked him.
Sir Norman was a man's man, and only spoke in monosyllables.
He was very gruff and shy and terrified of women,
much preferring his pipe. Annabel gave him
his favourite tobacco for his forty-fifth birthday.
His eyes seemed to light up with a brief understanding.

Myfanwy was a bit of a minx but everyone loved her.
A madcap girl who rode tractors side-saddle
and was on good terms with all the farmhands,
she nevertheless used to split the infinitive
and her spelling was atrocious. Annabel often
wondered if she would ever pass her 'O' Level English –
though she thought she might do well as a liberated woman,
with all that money. Annabel herself came
from the large family of an impoverished clergyman.
She was cheerful but indigent.

Time went by, and one day succeeded another.
At a party in the nearby market town,
to which Annabel had been invited by accident,
she met Sebastian Anchovy, a sophisticated novelist
and a member of another old County family –
carried away by an impulse and without really meaning to,
she took his side in an argument with Emery Sandpiper,
the Cockney critic, very brash and abrasive from his TV appearances,
who was saying how Margaret Drabble was really thick.

Annabel bristled with offended sensibility
and Sebastian said calmly: 'I beg to differ.'
Later he slipped her a joint in the bathroom
and they achieved a certain *rapport* of fellow feeling,
as he explained to her how Oxford wasn't Cambridge.

After that they continued to meet fairly often.
For afternoons together they would go off cycling,
wobbling through the primroses. Once Sebastian
laid a hand on her knee as they sat in a tea room.
Annabel knew he was beginning to care for her.
He even came to Stoatswold, and talked about
    shorthorns.
They would all three be sitting, with glasses of cowslip
    wine
(Myfanwy, the tomboy, was out shooting rabbits
in the company of a ferret called Fred),
and Sebastian would discourse at length about his
    ancestors.
Sir Norman said nothing, but carefully refilled his pipe.
In these conversations he was a kind of smoke-screen,
under cover of which Sebastian made advances.

Finally Annabel allowed him to kiss her.
They became engaged – but were keeping it secret
because of his mother, old Lady Anchovy.
Sir Norman was silent but seemed rather moody –
you could never tell what he was thinking.
Myfanwy had a crush on a cowhand called Joe
and was oblivious to everything that happened around
    her.

Nothing did happen – which was standard and
par for the course, as Sebastian might have said
in his civilized manner. Until one evening,
when Sir Norman had certainly taken
far more cowslip wine than was really good for him,
he dropped a pipe and broke it. 'Oh, flip!' he shouted.
Annabel was amazed to hear him swearing –
he was the sort of man who says 'Ladies present!' –

so she stared at him. 'What are you staring at,
you sly little puss?!' Sir Norman bellowed.
'I've seen you with Sebastian in the rhododendrons!'

Annabel caught a hanky to her eyes and rushed from the
    room.
At breakfast the next morning, over his scrambled eggs,
Sir Norman apologized. Later that day
he brushed against her, accidentally, in a passage.
Annabel felt the blood rising to her face. Abruptly
he seized her. 'Oh, Annabel! My darling!
How can I live without you?' Impulsively
he strained her to him. His moustache on her forehead
tickled her slightly – but quickly she realized
how her feeling for Sebastian was terribly superficial.
'Let me think!' she riposted; and half an hour later
the engagement was broken; and in the late summer
she became Lady Stoatswold. And in her honour
Myfanwy changed the name of her favourite ferret
and called her Annabel – she was the wife of Fred.

Sonnet: Brief Encounter

Did we really make that journey to Northampton?
In pursuit of that coloured abortionist who did the first
    one?
He was very nice, you said, and had a cocktail cabinet,
and seemed clean. Two children, you said,
were quite enough for one lifetime – though I don't think
    any
of this did you much good, physically. I waited an hour
in the Station buffet. Then you came back, suffering
a state of shock, shivering. I bought you a whisky.

76

I did some shoe advertising once for a firm in
 Northampton.
Northampton is where they make shoes. They're
 fertility symbols
(think of the old woman who lived in a shoe).
They're wombs and vaginas. 'Something you put your
 foot in'
I remember hearing a psychiatrist, once, say.
You felt very cold, in the train back to London.

The Semantic Limerick According to the Shorter Oxford English Dictionary (1933)

There existed an adult male person who had lived a
relatively short time, belonging or pertaining to St
John's,* who desired to commit sodomy with the large
web-footed swimming birds of the genus *Cygnus* or
subfamily *Cygninae* of the family *Anatidae*, characterized
by a long and gracefully curved neck and a majestic
motion when swimming.

So he moved into the presence of the person employed
to carry burdens, who declared: 'Hold or possess as
something at your disposal my female child! The large
web-footed swimming-birds of the genus *Cygnus* or sub-
family *Cygninae* of the family *Anatidae*, characterized by a
long and gracefully curved neck and a majestic motion
when swimming, are set apart, specially retained for the
Head, Fellows and Tutors of the College!'

* A College of Cambridge University.

77

Sonnet: The Womansmell of Sex

It's interesting how the sexual smell of women,
when they are excited by the touching of their lovers,
has never found its way into romantic literature
(nor, for that matter, into any other literature).
One poem by Donne. I can't think of much else.
The taboo must be very strong. Even pornography
describes visual and tactile but not the olfactory.
Some readers would go mad if it were even mentioned.

Of course, you can't describe a smell. Yet even
   hypocrites
would admit that for a man in love
this is an important factor in the physical attraction.
It should have, as it were, at least a footnote.
People don't like admitting that they're animals –
they turn their minds away from the fact and its proving.

1980-1982

Exits

If you imagine life as a large room,
most of the Exits are marked Painful –
and this is what causes fear,
to get from here to there
the despot, the dandy and the duffer
all have to suffer.

But with the sudden atomic boom –
this is what makes some men disdainful
of death – or the slick quick knife
or shot, you're out of life
like that! bingo! couldn't be faster!
And that's no disaster.

It's when the slow darknesses loom,
the clouds look doom-laden and rainful,
the lightning hysterias fly
across the agonized sky.
Long illness brings dreams of funerals, hearses –
but sudden death: mercies.

Don't mourn them, like some stolid marble tomb,
those who go out like a light – gainful
it isn't, and they had luck,
missed what we all would duck
if we'd the choice: feeling iller and iller.
Long live the instant killer!

25A Norfolk Crescent

It's odd to think how
in that once-untenanted space
above our house
a man is having a bath,
a man and a woman are making love,
life is going on
in what once was air.

In that block of luxury flats
nobody knows now where
the nursery was;
it's so easy to blame
my father's 'I'm very disappointed in you'
for ambition
and the feeling lost.

Mothers comfort. Too much;
and in Cambridge Square
two twin boys
were learning to be queers.
'As the twig is bent', they say,
it's all written,
they say, or in the stars.

The intelligent children
understand the insults –
they suffer most.
The dim ones just grin.
If I had imagination – too much –
my father none,
that was my bad luck.

At this distance in time
the fear and hate exist
but can't be touched –
that house is now a ghost
within a house, where others now
live and suffer.
Tall in the anxious air.

In the Restaurant

At the tables there is laughter, where executives are
    lunching.
'You're so beautiful!' a man says; there is holding hands
    (and footlove)
as the dishes and the egos, with experimental cooking,
so exaggerate the meetings and the matings of the
    twosomes.
All percentages and products are examined in the aura
of the wine carafes of redness that emblazon on the table
just the pinkness of the patches where white cloth is
    wobbled over –
as the sun that is our sovereign shines enticingly deep
    through them.

But the lovers and the agents, all of them demand a
    profit –
it may come in cheques, or simply the wet warmth of
    something fluffy.
For the laughter and the lovetalk are by no means, here,
    unselfish,
there is no one in the world who won't seek his own
    advantage
or seek hers (and I must say this); every altruistic action
is itself a conscience-soother and still has its private
    audience
of a God who sits in judgment, or more public
    approbation.
All the women stroke men's torsos for their own delight
    and sharing.

There's a two-way traffic running even in the kissing
    glances
of a girl who eyes a loved one over plates of fegatoni.
Even gold-diggers are giving, in a sense it's all a bargain.
See the black and busty hustle of the waitresses,
    good-natured
in the face of many orders; they are paid, of course, to do
    it.

It's so true we all want something – and that something
   might be someone –
that the only problem left is: do we do it sad, or gaily?
restaurants are no exception, and the whole of life is
   business.

Sestina: The Literary Gathering

At one end of the peculiar table Jeremy
sat, and talked about poetry to Carl.
He was a bit of a nutter. Next to him, Sheila
was eating a farinaceous dish. Lewis
listened intently to the words of Ursula.
They were all drinking cider. And so was Jane.

There was something quiet and achieved about Jane –
of course she was a good deal older than Lewis –
and she hadn't got the manic quality of Jeremy
nor did she understand engineering, like Carl,
or the details of catering, which obviously Ursula
had at her fingertips. They all liked Sheila.

They all agreed there was no one like Sheila
for lovability. Music to Jeremy
was the breath of life. Often, to Carl,
he would play his autoharp – this delighted Ursula
and certainly caused some pleasure to Jane –
sitting in the meadow with the cows and Lewis.

'Lewis?' said Jane. 'He's a dark horse, Lewis!'
'You never know what he's thinking!' cried Sheila.
'He's a very nice boy' was the verdict of Ursula;
he seemed more ordinary to Carl and Jeremy.
He was fond of Milton (he once told Jane) –
but only modern poets appealed to Carl.

There was a hint of dark Satanic mills about Carl,
a contained intelligence; no fly-by-night Jeremy,
he hadn't the open character of Ursula,
in this respect he was more like Jane
or the sheep and the cattle. And only Sheila
seemed to understand him – except for Ursula.

There was a bardic bravery about Ursula.
Not even Lewis, or Jane, or Sheila
had her bravura – in the words of Lewis
'She is the mother of us all!' For Jane
Ursula's writing was the tops, and Carl
confessed he was staggered, and even Jeremy,

though he liked Carl and respected Jane
and admired Lewis (and the work of Sheila),
said how he, Jeremy, really worshipped Ursula.

Circe I

Her Caliban cunt
was wild and woolly,
her nipples like
the ends of lemons,
she was an expert on
all kinds of pigfood.

For the rough sailors
she poured the wine out,
but for one man only
she plumped satin cushions,
spreading her bum,
inviting him in.

He felt so special,
a wonderful lover,
superior grunting
in bowers of vine-leaves;
pigs their background
and love their pigfood.

84

'Ce Petit Détail, Tellement Sexuel'

– Romain Rolland, *Le Six Octobre*

In the old days you were seriously worshipped,
carved on temples, always a prominent feature
of certain gods in gardens, propped in an upright position
on dead bodies of the Pharaohs;

secretly, the obelisks all celebrated you –
even the Victorians in Kensington Gardens
with the Speke Memorial obliquely remembered you –
and the spires of all the churches.

Jocular and lewd you exist at Pompeii
along with the scales and the Roman soldier
and all through the South small facsimiles of you
keep the Evil Eye from harming,

an Italian under-culture; and it's not surprising
that the word 'fascinate' (which belonged to the witches)
in the Greek and the Latin had its first meaning:
render impotent. Late Horace

used *fascinum* to mean you. You remain worrying
to all Puritans, and you can really frighten
bossy middle-aged busybodies. Like Armageddon,
truthfully they fear to see you.

Some religions impose a strict taboo
as rigid and inflexible as yourself; and detailed
representation in works of art, illegal,
is almost everywhere forbidden.

This is the bad news. There's a lot of it –
but I bring you too a modified message of hope.
As long as we exist, I think, in secret
your cult, enthusiastic twosomes

bowing down before you (as they always did),
will prosper; for the worshipping millions
in a real sense still owe their existence to you –
not quite a god, but a bold symbol.

An Old Husband Suspects Adultery

I was just beginning to feel in the mood,
my desire was just beginning to harden,
as we lay cuddling like Babes in the Wood
or Adam and Eve naked in that Garden –
when the telephone started ringing.
She jumped out of bed (like Eve, naked)
and answered it – I could hear him darlinging.

She spoke to him coolly but she wasn't rude,
taking it in her stride with her long legs – flustered
she certainly wasn't. No thought of Bad or Good
grazed her. Domestic as custard
she talked, as if to a grocer,
like smooth-limbed Eve with a handset, naked,
standing there beautiful. I was feeling moroser

than I can tell you. A pin-up, a nude,
she'd made herself. Unreachable. She hung up
and climbed back into bed. Like Robin Hood
he'd robbed the rich – before he'd rung up
I'd really felt like doing it,
but now the thread was lost – Eve, so naked, couldn't
tempt me now into pursuing it.

A Contemporary Film of Lancasters in Action

To see them bombing up
and wheeling off into the dusk,
nose to tail, queueing, turning for the take-off,
like long-jumpers each one coming up
stationary
before they begin the run before the jump,
piloted by volunteer bank clerks.
Is my emotion bogus or inflationary?

I was never a hero,
the shark's tooth, boar's tusk,
seeming less frightening than this kind of flying,
for all kinds of courage rated zero,
admiringly
I admit they did what I could never,
sleepwalkers showing a sleepless courage –
long flights to firework climax, untiringly.

Obstinate, I survive
and, writing in this summer musk,
I say they were the patient venturing lions
and I the mean dog that stayed alive;
we owe them
every valedictory mark of respect
(bravery's facing such boring dangers)
that we can possibly, too late, show them.

A 14-Year Old Convalescent Cat in the Winter

I want him to have another living summer,
to lie in the sun and enjoy the *douceur de vivre* –
because the sun, like golden rum in a rummer,
is what makes an idle cat *un tout petit peu ivre* –

I want him to lie stretched out, contented,
revelling in the heat, his fur all dry and warm,
an Old Age Pensioner, retired, resented
by no one, and happinesses in a beelike swarm

to settle on him – postponed for another season
that last fated hateful journey to the vet
from which there is no return (and age the reason),
which must soon come – as I cannot forget.

Conversation Piece

I sit and hear my mother and my aunt
talking of dog-carts, of a century gone
I try to imagine (there are some who can't).
Their total age is 181.
Under the clothes, the bodies were the same
as those the striptease, shamelessly as cards,
deals to the watchers now. Just the same game
but played by different rules; *ripostes, on guards*,

masks of all sorts, the flirting with a fan,
a kind of fencing with an instinct. Who loved who
they had their ways of knowing, woman and man.
Something outside them told them what to do.

They weren't direct like us (are we direct?),
Victoria sat there like a monolith
but even nice girls knew what to expect,
how Zeus crept up on Leda in the myth –

without a visiting card, in fancy dress.
No lady left the house without her gloves.
Deafness makes meaning something they must guess,
arthritis stiffens Venus and her doves,
for four decades no lovemaking at all –
beauty was jolly, with a motoring veil.
There should be writing, writing on the wall:
All sex shall fail, but love shall never fail.

The Late Eighties

To her
I am a coloured blur,
   a just-heard voice,
   as she sits there –
she hasn't any choice.

Life fades
like on-off hearing aids,
   and in her sleep
   the realler world
is dreaming, long and deep.

This now
needs living through somehow,
   patience is all
   and the time left,
though slow, is surely small.

        I touch
the body changed so much,
    she understands
    some tenderness
through bony arms and hands.

        Contact
is joining and a fact;
    we once were one,
    and touching's how
all lovemaking gets done.

On First Looking into Michael Grant's Cities of Vesuvius

In battledress, yes, I was there. That dramatic great
                            wartime eruption
    spewed out the red-hot shit; it looked very splendid
                            at night
crushing the villas and trees, and the ash came down, a
                            red-purple,
    to the depth of an old-fashioned foot. We moved the
                            trucks and the guns
for safety. But our letters home were security-minded.
                            No mention.
    You needed a four-wheel drive to churn through
                            that stuff on the road.
This was in March '44 (as the clubland talks would
                            remind you),
    of Europe's one active volcano the last recorded
                            display.

Before this happened, I took, on an outing, a party of
                                        gunners
    (we weren't operational then) to Pompeii; they
                            wanted the church,
the wine-shops, the cheap souvenirs. I opted, alone, for
                                    the *Scavi*.
        I had one guide to myself – and paid with a tin of
                                corned beef.
We covered a lot of the ground. His English was good
                            but not perfect –
        I was pleased to hear of a king whose name seemed
                        to be Charles the Turd.
Although I went there three times – with a friend on
                                two visits –
    and the guide remarked with a grin, as we looked at
                    the rough plaster thighs,
how it was obvious enough that the body we saw was a
                                    woman.
    We went round the brothel as well. He lit up the
                        paintings on walls
with a candle held high; you could see where each girl's
                        speciality, pictured
    above the door of her room, enticed you inside to
                            her skill.
He unlocked for us, too, with his key, that famous and
                        frivolous fresco
    which shows the soldier who weighs his huge
                    uncircumcised cock
on the scales, and the gold goes up – for pleasure's more
                        precious than money.
    Behind us, by accident, there (for this is inside a
                            house door)
an American nurse walked by. She gave a great 'Oo!' and
                            fled, shaken.
    I don't know what it's like now. But *Off Limits*
                    would, then, be the words;
and the delicate souls of the girls were protected, the
                    brothel was banned; though
    plain enough in the road you could see a large
                        bas-relief tool
to point the vernacular way to the house dedicated to
                                    Venus.

With a naked foot, on dark nights, it must have been
useful, at that.
Herculaneum wasn't so good. The best thing of all was
the statue
that shows Pan at work on a goat. This was our
verdict, at least.

So, Grant, you swim into my ken. With your writing, so
large and clear, telling
of thirty-three years ago now – more or less, give or
take, to the day
when the boil on the neck of the land burst, on the
warlike eighteenth
and we stood with our drinks, there, to watch, on
the roof of the officers' mess,
how the lava rolled down in the dark, a slow raw mass on
the skyline.
We didn't think so much, then, of the suffering; how
those who died
choked in the chemical fumes – like the brave and
inquisitive Pliny,
like the dog at the end of its chain. That's one of the
things about war.
The dying was commonplace, then. It was interesting,
more than distressing.
And of course you're entirely right, the gladiatorial
shows
were disgusting (as Seneca said); more so than the
drinking and fucking.
Dr Arnold, the father, who wrote that the Bay of
Naples was one
long drama (and 'fearsome' too) of Sin and Death, and,
yes, Pleasure,
got it wrong in his Puritan way – and so did his
talented son.
Why should there be shame? No one lived (as you say) to
be much over forty –
over most of the world, to this day, that's an average
life.

We are exceptions, aloof and well-dressed in our
                                        self-conscious cities.
    If any small British town, perhaps a resort like
                                        Torquay,
were quickly hermetically sealed, volcanoed and covered
                                        for ever,
        would archaeologists find such a high standard of
                                        art?
Architecture, as well. I think you make a good point
                                        there.
        I know they crucified slaves. There was cruelty, but
                                        easiness too;
the easiness of a land where the passions could be quite
                                        volcanic
    but with the blue sea and sky there was always
                                        benevolent sun.

The Moment

There are even photographs of it:
the moment when, for the first time,
in that tense, expectant landscape,
the enemy troops appear.

There they are, advancing –
Germans from World War One
running with rifles.
As, from far back in time, so many others.

You are the opposing infantry –
this means you.
Your brain falters. *This
is it*, you think,

*these are the ones we've heard
so much about.* Like old people
when, for the first time, they confront
the unambiguous symptoms.

Pian dei Giullari

Never go back, they say. Never go back.
I went back.

With my twenty-one-year-old daughter
I walked through the Porta Romana,
up the Erta Canina,
round the curved Giramonte
and high beyond the city.

I was twice as old as then.
A lot of it I didn't recognize,
I thought we were lost –
till a name startled me into recognition:
Pian dei Giullari.
A small hilly road
but there, as in sentimental dreams,
was the straight drive through the olive orchard,
the house in faded orange with barred windows,
our once Headquarters.

And there, almost opposite,
the entrance to her villa
where 28 embraced 16.

Was this sad or happy?

Our weak, nice Major died
(I saw his obituary by accident),
the love affair came to nothing.

In those days we were careless –
as the war was careless of us.
Nobody thought very far ahead.
Girls were like wine for the drinking.

The landscape that we saw from our windows
in a time of cicadas and nightingales
stood there unaltered.
I looked at it and felt the warm lightness
of khaki drill on my shoulders.

The Dying Animals

The animals that look at us like children
in innocence, in perfect innocence!
The innocence that looks at us! Like children
the animals, the simple animals,
have no idea why legs no longer work.

The food that is refused, the love of sleeping –
in innocence, in childhood innocence
there is a parallel of love. Of sleeping
they're never tired, the dying animals;
sick children too, whose play to them is work.

The animals are little children dying,
brash tigers, household pets – all innocence,
the flames that lit their eyes are also dying,
the animals, the simple animals,
die easily; but hard for us, like work!

Sonnet: The Greedy Man Considers Nuclear War

I suppose you all realize we shall lose the sizzling sausages
and the mild mountains of mashed potatoes!
Boiled silverside with dumplings, raspberries and cream!
We shall vanish from the pecking order of the tikka
    chicken,
trout with almonds will swim away from us,
little lambs no more will jump into our mouths,
fragrant with rosemary; all the good wholesome food
will vanish just as surely as sophisticated dishes!

And what shall we be left with? Some assorted politicians
not very good to eat, some dispirited root crops,
tinned food perhaps – everything else burned up,
the culture of the kitchen, the chef's wisdom of the ages
vanished in a flame like the bread in a toaster!
The end of eating civilization as we know it!

Sonnet: The Red Fairy Book

I remember as a child I used to be terrified
by the illustrations to those stories that Andrew Lang
    collected,
where Princes were likely to be chopped into little pieces,
something nasty lived in the lake, and nine-headed Trolls
were decapitated by some good-hearted simpleton.
There was also a horrible Japanese animal
that spoke when it was cut into joints that hung from the
    ceiling
and because of its pleading was finally reconstituted and
    dangerous. . . .

96

But in fact the real world, now that I know it,
turns out to be quite a good deal more horrible –
where men are skinned alive and castrated,
where various emblems are stuck into women,
there's self-righteous torture (electric chairs and
    hanging).
And nothing can be remedied, as in fairy stories.

Sonnet: Comics

The comics know their way about (they always have),
they know they can raise the giggling laugh by saying
'He has very heavy commitments', 'He's got a large
    overdraft'
or 'Take down her particulars!' It's standard,
oblique references to cocks, balls, breasts, even (by way
    of pussies)
cunts. And this is how the Puritans like it,
it's exactly like scratching something that itches
(hence prurience); it's sly and not direct. Though
    pleasurable.

But if you use the words, describe the actions, they go up
    in flames.
Somehow they are not easy (we are not easy)
about being sexual creatures. They won't accept
that at best we're thinking animals. So keep it dark.
The preachers and the comics are in league.
Creating and dispersing thoughts of guilt.

Sonnet: The Light and the Dark

You say: Why are all the poems about the dark side of
  marriage?
About the rows, the screaming, the differences of
  opinion.
I say (because I like arguing?) that very few of them are –
but in any case poems are general and not to be
  interpreted literally
and they're also a kind of cure for the bad parts of life.
Stating a problem is itself, in a way, a solution.
Happiness is the one emotion a poem can't capture,
there are very few sonnets that purr with contentment.

But here goes! To be in a warm bed with somebody
  friendly,
to be looked after, cooked for, cared for; these are not
  nothings.
Conversation and fun, companionship, Twenty
  Questions,
humming the Verdi, Puccini, Bellini. ... .
Do I have to write it out in words: *I love you*,
after the fondness of a quarter of a century?

The Victorian Husband
(Before the Murder)

Each morning, coffee cold as ice,
His thoughts to one thought carried:
How nice to be happily married,
To be married to somebody nice!

With mangled muffins and bad tea,
As insults were being parried,
He thought: To be happily married,
To be married to someone like me!

If I were rich – that would suffice!
I should not be so harried.
I should be happily married
To somebody really nice!

The Meeting

In the long and boring meeting,
in the hot and boring meeting,
there was shouting by the Chairman,
bullying almost by the Chairman,
people rose on points of order,
caused chaos with points of order,
argument became emotive,
all the words used were emotive,
and this was the obvious reason
passion overcame all reason.

Everything was twice repeated,
sometimes more than twice repeated,
as they worked through the agenda
(it seemed elastic, that agenda,
becoming longer, never shorter),
their utterances grew long, not shorter,
it was just like spreading butter,
words went further, like spread butter,
covering each subject thinly,
covering almost nothing thinly.

People talked about resigning,
disgruntled talk was of resigning,
accusations in a covey
flew like partridge in a covey,
yet this was not entertaining –
it sounds like drama, entertaining
as the TV scenes in courtrooms –
this was *not* like scenes in courtrooms,
it contrived to be quite boring,
really quite immensely boring.

It was more like scenes where children
shout insults at other children,
it was like a verbal punch-up,
more long-winded than a punch-up,
but the bitterness and anger
brought out words like knives in anger,
it was more like verbal murder
if there's boredom in a murder –
any moderate survivors
in the end *felt* like survivors.

Like being rescued from a snowstorm,
or blinding words whirled like a snowstorm;
they could only cry for brandy,
go to pubs and order brandy,
they felt they deserved some medals
like the Army's campaign medals –
through the tumult and the shouting
(quiet was strange after the shouting)
they achieved the peace of something
through the meeting – which was something.

It was like peace after beating
heads on walls, like hours of beating
heads on walls and never stopping –
till at last the joy of stopping
seemed a truly great achievement,
lack of pain, a great achievement,
it's so lovely when you stop it!
Negative delight, to stop it,
flooded through them after meeting
at that long hot boring meeting!

They Flee from Me
That Sometime Did Me Seek

At this moment in time
the chicks that went for me
in a big way
are opting out;
as of now, it's an all-change situation.

The scenario was once,
for me, 100% better.
Kissing her was viable
in a nude or semi-nude situation.
It was *How's about it, baby?*,
her embraces were relevant
and life-enhancing.

I was not hallucinating.
But with regard to that one
my permissiveness
has landed me in a forsaking situation.
The affair is no longer on-going.
She can, as of now, explore new parameters –
How's about it? indeed!
I feel emotionally underprivileged.
What a bitch!
(and that's meaningful!).

Crucifixion

Suppose they came along one morning and said 'Right! To-day we're going to crucify you!' It would come as a shock, to say the least; and particularly if they had already set up a brand new wooden cross, handmade, in your back garden, and had the hammers and high quality nails ready, no expense spared, to do the thing in style. After the first numbness of the shock, who would be able to resist shouting and screaming, completely hysterical or even technically mad? There would certainly be fainting and falling about. We forget too easily how such cruelty was once commonplace, no more regarded than (nowadays) a starving lost dog in the harsh streets of a big city. The man or woman who could contemplate the endurance of such torture – for they would not hesitate to crucify women, and even children – with the calm and philosophical courage advised by the Ancients would be rare indeed.

1982-1985

The Young Pobble's Guide to his Toes

Everything comes, everything goes.
Some day you must say goodbye to your toes –
all bitten off by the beasts of the sea
or fading away by a gradual degree,
vanishing into an elbowless night
all blurred and dim in your elderly sight.
The sun goes down and the eyes give up,
your toes will fade, kerflip, kerflup . . .

The moral shines bright as a mermaid's hair.
Count them and keep them while they're still there!

Lights Out

With each new book the old poet thinks:
Will this be the last?
Biros, pencils, typewriters, pens and inks
whisper to him: Get going! Move!
Get it out fast!

Cram the poems in like a herring glut –
two, three to the page!
Randify your writing, riot and rut,
time's short, get out of that groove
they call old age!

Write it all down, write it fast and loose,
it may be sad stuff –
and you were never a golden egg goose –
but shout it out, coming too soon you've
got silence enough!

Singable

Maimed personalities make the best poets still,
with flaws all over the shop,
opium and alcohol, no one could say of them
they never touched a drop –
and there's a strain of reclusive old ladies too
who hardly go out to tea,
agoraphobes, with a murderous loneliness –
not jolly, like you and me –
all the neurotics, the Muse will quite welcome them,
yes, *and* their queerness and quirks,
what does it matter? It turns out so singable,
it doesn't gum up the works!

Aros Castle

I first saw Aros Castle when I was ten, in 1926 –
a ruin with a great ruined window like an eye.
My father took me shooting rabbits. I can fix

all that in my mind. There was a man with a ferret,
the rabbits lived under the rocks, quite near the shore.
I shot my first-ever rabbit. I was proud with acquired
                                        merit.

And on the small headland the Castle sat still,
looking like a picture postcard view from a window.
After that summer I didn't see it again until

I came to Mull in 1937 (I was twenty-one),
I was reading *Present Indicative*, I'd just finished
                                        Cambridge,
I had no job in prospect, a lot remained to be done,

it was hot and we drove Margery's car round the
                                        island roads,
Calgary, Gribun and so on, a lovely summer,
and the Castle still sat there like something with loads

of time on its hands. The eye never blinked or
                                        shifted.
It stood there clear. If it vanished, it would come
                                        back –
as soon as the rain stopped or the mist lifted.

When (in 1967?) I saw it again
I had Margo with me, it was Easter,
a huge rabbit popped up and eyed us with disdain

outside the window, at breakfast. The world had
                                        carried
on with its wars and its worries, the Castle
                                        notwithstanding,
and I had been eleven years married.

That eye never closed. It wasn't designed for sleeping.
It seemed (perhaps this is the pathetic fallacy)
as though it had Time or something in its own
safe keeping.

In 1968 we brought the kids before its unchanging
face.
Jane had to dive into Tobermory Bay from a boat
among a lot of jellyfish. It was part of a race.

And this year, 1981, was (so far) the last time.
I once walked to the Castle – its base is smothered in
nettles
and walking round it isn't much of a pastime.

I think it's nearly 500 years old, but I might be
wrong.
Obviously someone once took trouble to destroy it –
it's a long time since, as a castle, it was really on
song!

Man and boy, you might say, I've been there and
seen it,
as tourist and time-traveller. If they holocaust us
(if Reagan and the Russians really mean it)

I bet that crumbling picturesque dump outlasts us!
Meanwhile it's into thoughtfulness, if not depression,
that that non-seeing picture postcard eye creepily casts

The Good Companions

They stand behind you and whisper:
Fill your glass! and *Fill your plate!*
Now they are nameless, but later you'll know their
names,
fiends and familiars with eating and drinking games:
Big Belly and Red Nose and Brain Damage.
They'll find you, sure as fate!

Tip-tankards, they jog the elbow:
Let's finish it! Have the other half!
They'll be your companions throughout your later
life,
the Knights of the Blissful Bottle, the Knavish Knife,
Lord Blood Pressure, Lady Redvein-Cheeknet,
the lewd litre, the loud laugh!

I could do with a drink! they whisper,
Oh, for a knife! Oh, for a fork!
Though they're refined gourmets and eat a lot of
French
you'll know them by a very piglike kind of stench,
Lady Burper, Bad Breath, Fartwell –
all dying for the popping of a cork!

In Another Country

Our bodies have changed
and are no longer the same
as those that had connection
a quarter century ago;

the scar by the nipple
where the cancer was excised,
the blotch where radiation
burned sore the tender skin;

the womb quite removed;
and a grey white streak
badgers your forehead –
though you still sing in tune.

I too am altering;
fatness and falling hair,
grey at the temples;
wartlike excrescences

appear on my back,
on my arms and legs;
grave-marks on hands.
I'm more like an old frog

than I ever used to be,
twinged by arthritis,
gout warnings in toes.
I have more in common

with our vintage cat
than with the children.
All this is not amazing
in a life where old poets

retire into envy
and drink themselves to death
among their admirers
in out-of-the-way places.

Ageing is a faintness
like a line in Shakespeare:
old, old, old, old.
Say it over and over.

In the Old People's Home (1914)

This is the last anchorage. HMS *Incontinent*
is in trouble and signals of distress
come from HMS *Repetitive* and HMS *Wanderer*.
HMS *Anxiety* is getting steam up.
The harbour is full of signs of activity,
which are all ignored by HMS *Vainglorious*
as she rides at anchor in perpetual majesty.

Across the water, puffing busily,
come the officious tugs *Snapper* and *Orderly*.

Boom Christmas

Because the people of Britain know that the end is
                                           nigh
and the Instruments of Satan are already installed on
                                      our shores,
they go mad for the Good Life, for the glass and the
                              food and the thigh,
lusting after Consumer Goods like kerb-crawlers after
                                      whores . . .

They know this is their Last Chance, it may not come
                                      round again,
they know the sizzling turkeys may well be the Final
                                           Birds
and each one knows what's fried may possibly be his
                                           brain,
as the comforting Christmas carols ascend in their
                              fifths and thirds . . .

And all this is traditional, in times of great Dying and
                                          Plague,
like the Fornication on Tombstones and the
                        Drunkenness in the Streets,
it's a clear indication of a Giant Despair, it's not in
                                  any way vague –
now it means bodies in plastic bags, as once it meant
                                  winding sheets.

Cruel and Unusual Punishments

How a masochist must long for the electric chair!
The wonderful bondage of his/her hands and feet,
the claustrophobic hood fitting over the face,
the metal cap so snug on the shaven cranium,
the plate on the shin and best of all
o best of all
the gagging effect of the mouthpiece –
so leather and lovely
that Spinkelink, asked for his last statement,
could only say 'I can't speak!'
which the Governor elected to take for his last
                                          statement.

Surely one could find volunteers to be electrocuted!
Just as people who agitate to bring back hanging
are always writing in for the job of hangman
or, it may even be, of hangwoman;
they are the sadists, the positives to that negative.

Towards the End of a Novel of 1910: A Passionate Outburst

For nearly a full year
these were the words I dearly longed to hear!
I love you – when you said them in the conservatory,
with the clashing billiard balls just audible
and later the doomful and ominous gong
as it were spreading the news, for from that little
                            statement
grows a great volume of sound,
church choirs, responses, vows, vows and vows!

I waited so very long
for those few stuttering notes to burst into song!
I love you – from the prominent bosom and the
                         narrow-waisted gown
that constricted your softness, I accepted it,
the sigh from your head on my shoulder,
like a waft of cigar scent on some dark summer
                          terrace
it flavoured the warmth of the night,
giving rise to events, a smoke message,
                    important . . .

I had faith and belief,
like a beleaguered town that daily expects relief!
I love you – I knew I should hear it from the
                     finger-traced lips
and I revolved it in my mind like the
dark brown brandy in the glass,
a pleasure to come, a delight to be savoured,
a future enclosed in a phrase,
so we could go forward like trains at signals greening!

Robert Graves

When Robert Graves got involved
with a wildly unsuitable woman
his problems were *not* solved –

though he, later, did get married
to a much more suitable woman.
But he was considerably harried

by an arrogant arid virago –
a madly unsuitable woman.
If he'd sailed off in an Argo

like Jason, and left them all screaming
(each clearly unsuitable woman),
it might have been better – but dreaming

of Goddesses (White) and of Muses
(the *younger* unsuitable woman)
is what the male masochist chooses!

O Governesses and O Nurses!
From the strains of Unsuitable Woman
came the excellence of his verses!

Only a Few Thousand Can Play

Poetry is a very ancient indoor game
like chess and draughts and knucklebones;
it can arouse emotion, it can be fun,
but you must always remember the galaxies
where the writ of T.S. Eliot does not run,

and the streets that are full of don't-knows
with other ways of using spare time;
verse-writing is a hobby, or a craft,
pursued by the uncommitted singleton
who into a great sea launches his raft,

not knowing quite where he will land or how,
if the rough rhymes will hold the logs in place
or the dovetailing stand the tall waves.
It's only then that the artificer
sees how, in rough weather, it behaves.

Deathbeds

In the old days when people died
the whole family gathered round the bed
standing or kneeling (patriarchal or matriarchal)
and the last frail blessings and goodbyes were
                                    said . . .
and people also said things like 'His race is nearly run'
and 'Fear no more the heat o' the sun',

and the old cock had fallen into desuetude
and the womb no longer wept its blood –
yet the children stood there (filial and familial)
by the upright grandfather clock's sad ticking thud,
and everybody's tears made it an occasion not to be
                                    missed
as the last dutiful kisses were kissed . . .

but now they are spirited away, behind curtains,
hidden in hospitals, wrapped warm in drugs,
they don't see the kids for whom (paternal or
                                    maternal)
they had the love; and solitary, slower than slugs,
the unconscious hours move past them. Nobody
                                    wants to know
or cares exactly when they go . . .

114

Father Love

To see you standing there, a great big beautiful son,
twenty-three years old and back from two months in
                                        America,
gave me a pang; it was love, it was seeing a vision,
it was what Margo your mother was obviously
                                feeling, with kisses;
for women, in spite of the Sisters, can have sons and
                                love them.
But men kissing and holding aren't really part of our
                                        culture.
It's the slap on the back, something more than a
                                handshake
yet not as emotional as the arms-round embrace.
I stood there. I was happy – but I never touched you.
I was pleased, I was proud as a parent, I said 'Hello,
                                fruitcake!'
or some other greeting, banal from the Marx Brothers
                                thirties . . .

That's the way it takes us, but it wasn't always so.
There were days of no stiff upper lip and no biting
                                back tears.

America, some say, is a big crooked country
and has been since the Volstead Act and Jesus Saves
got it organized for crime (with what good
                                intentions!) –
but you weren't coming back from the dead or some
                                Ultima Thule,
although I suppose you could have been shot by a
                                lunatic.

So perhaps emotion wasn't in place; but, once, men
                                wept openly
and threw their arms about, hugging the prodigals
and squeezing the loved ones, both breathless and
                                tearful.

I think the Greeks did, and even the Romans
who thought fairly highly, their books say, of
                                        hardness
and all the republican virtues. They did, yes, I think
                                        they did.

We are so used to the thought that nothing is perfect.
A novelist invents a most attractive girl with a nose
                                        like a ski jump
and we know for certain that (as with the moon)
                                there's always a dark side.
But this was unlooked for and happy, pure gold on
                                        the stream bed
or a delicious chocolate coming random from the
                                        box.

St Syphilis and All Devils

As I sit eating a Heinz Big Soup
I can hear the choir of St Syphilis and All Devils:
they are singing for me in a little chapel-of-ease,
part of the ruins of St Erysipelas-the-Less.
Big Nasties in their robes conduct the service.

The motorways are chill, and cold the concrete,
there is no nourishment in a spaghetti junction,
the foods and wines are trapped in cold tin
as everywhere the sleety rain comes down .
and all the cars whizz past like lions and demons.

Unemployed boys are freezing in disaster,
the frizzy-haired girls are cold as Eskimos,
everything is packaged, disaster is packaged,
human contacts are the taunts and stabbing,
dead boredom at home, outside the hellpacks . . .

And now they unwrap the little packaged wars
lodged in their tinsel at the foot of the Christmas tree,
there are little bangs and crackers; but the big presents
remain to the last. Who will get what? All the
                                            choristers
rise and explode in a giant crescendo . . .

Rusted iron in broken concrete and thin dead trees.
Clear on all the transistors that demonic choir
is singing enthusiastically of human breakdown,
fat fiends in surplices, St Syphilis and All Devils:
working for a profit, putting *us* in the collection.

Fair Women

When I was young
I used to see the
photographs in the paper
of the women for whom men
had seen fit to do murder:
big battleaxes or only half-pretty,
hauled into some court in some city.

They didn't seem
at all attractive –
photographs show most women
(at least the snapshotty ones)
not much apt to coax semen;
and in those prison-van circumstances
their charms didn't have the best of chances.

They weren't like stars
that gleamed on screens (like
shining-haired Joan Bennett);
with their supporting police
they were more like Mack Sennet,
bulging old bags, the targets for crowd hisses –
I couldn't imagine covering them with kisses.

117

But now I know
two people only,
always, are involved there –
and this is more of a mystery
than Holmes ever solved. There
is no place for cameras or other outsiders –
the only third person is Love, with her blazing
                                        outriders.

As each stood,
her V of hair dark,
so clearly, perfectly naked,
she seemed a goddess perhaps,
the man was proud to make it,

that love – the V between her legs a Y and furry,
her face in close-up (as photographed later) blurry . . .

On top of them
the men lay hard, and
sucked their pinksoft nipples
(they might have been terrible hags
or sluts – that view's other people's)
until long hatreds built up, or short quarrels,
to Death – nothing to do with photography or morals.

Did You See the Ace of Spades?

*Tilly told me lots of bitchy stories about Adele Astaire . . .
'She saw me with Friedrich and with Prince Obolensky;
she is very jealous of these two tall, handsome men; she is
so hot to get a man and is so unable to. She has quickies
with the stage-hands. She calls them into her dressing-room
and they have her on the floor.'*
*. . . I became rather cold towards Adele. She was rather
wild. I remember once in New York, she got out of my
Rolls-Royce on my side, by lifting her legs over the gear*

lever, and deliberately showing everything in so doing. She
saw the expression on my face and said, 'Oh, hello! Did
you see the ace of spades?'

– Edward James on Tilly Losch and Adele Astaire,
The Observer, 18 July 1982

Fred and Adele Astaire!
Like Mickey Mouse and Minnie Mouse,
the simple innocent dancers!
Lady, Be Good! was there,
written in lights, the Empire, Leicester Square –

the songs, but not the show
(1928 and I was twelve)
because of the gramophone records
I did indeed know!
They still carry a strong nostalgic glow.

And, later, *Funny Face*,
this one I certainly saw,
puberty's edge, or just after –
but the blood didn't race
in heart, pulse or that forfended place.

She simply seemed quite cute,
comic and with no hint,
as she tap-danced with her brother,
of old forbidden fruit,
diamonds, spades or any other suit . . .

It's nice to know, with age,
that she was human too
(though who trusts feminine gossip?),
sexy, out of the cage,
and lived where lionsize desires rage . . .

After those five decades,
and I'd never seen it then,
(she aristocratically married),
though all desire fades,
I know a lot more about the ace of spades.

The Town Mouse and the Country Mouse

The country poets – Thomas, Gurney, Clare –
loving the landscapes, treescapes, cloudscapes,
seem far removed (as Hodge from Fred Astaire)
from all the sly sophisticated Byrons
who delight only in a town's environs.
The Mount of Venus is the hill *they* see,
where every hair in close-up is a tree.

For city-dwellers fields are cold and wet –
and full of dimwits, rustics, clodhoppers,
though land means money (no Lord can forget).
In overlordship they were unforgiving
and Clare, we know, could barely scrape a living.
The prosperous farmer never saw much harm
in the forced labour of his prosperous farm.

Patrons and peasants both, they could agree
that land's not landscape, treescape, cloudscape.
Crops from the soil and apples from the tree,
all of it business, warlike, they were waging –
there was a price on what looked so engaging.
Romantic barren land was not much good;
except as timber, who could love a wood?

Sonnet: Equality of the Sexes

I'm sure if I were a woman I should hate
being regarded as someone designed by Nature
to answer the telephone, make sandwiches, make tea;
or be fucked, look after a family, wash, cook, sew.
I would want to be an engineer, I would want to be
                                                       regarded
as a person whose sex, though inescapable, was
                                                     accidental
and not of the first importance. Though we don't
                                                     deny
there *are* maternal feelings – and traces of
                                          masochism . . .

still, though men are in the rat race, and the American
                                              Satan
with not much help from others could burn us all up,
even so – if men are devils – we mustn't think all
                                              women
are perfect, downtrodden angels. There are nasty
                                        people about
of both sexes – surely you know some? Equally nasty
(or equally nice?) – that's one 'equality of the sexes'.

Sonnet: Supernatural Beings

You can't ever imagine the Virgin Mary having
                                        vulvitis or thrush –
she's not a real woman, she's a supernatural being,
not like the real women who are snoring and farting.
Aldous Huxley in an essay said that the angels
painted so often in Italian pictures
would need huge pectoral muscles if they were ever
                                        to fly . . .
But angels, like the Virgin, are supernatural beings.
It's all done by magic. If you can, you believe it.

And not so much *if you can*, more *if you want to* –
if you want to imagine something a bit kinder than
                                        people,
full of love and bursting with benevolence
you go for these smiling supernatural do-gooders
that look a little patronizing to an ordinary man
and still can't prevent you getting cancer or a cold.

Sonnet: Playing for Time

This was the telefilm of women in Auschwitz,
written by Arthur Miller, with Vanessa Redgrave
as the lean head-shaven French nightclub singer
in the camp orchestra – a great performance.
One critic called it Daughter of Holocaust
(a critic must have his little joke)
but it's only right we should be reminded
how racism persists right into the gas ovens (Jews
                                      and Poles)

though humanity, common to all, should bridge the
                         gap.
And how all these things did actually happen.
From stress and malnutrition they stopped
                           menstruating,
their shaved heads too made them look sexless –
they could have been men. All you could say was
(and this was perhaps the point) they all looked
                            human.

Sonnet: The Last Days

'Why have you put me here, underneath the earth?'
'You are still with us.'
'That cannot be. Beethoven is not here.'

     – Schubert in delirium, during his last illness

When you lie in a hospital, in an old folks' home, in
         your final illness,
all your defences are down. The brothers and sisters
         you didn't get on with
can visit you at will. Sly women who expect legacies
can come and knit by your bedside, buttering you up.
Boring women with tactless talk of the deaths of
         relatives –
the kind of friends you could do without – they all
         swarm round you.
Even looking at them makes you tired, let alone
         talking,
and you are scarcely protected by bossy nurses or
         matrons.

If you are one of the distressed gentlefolk who live
         into their nineties
in a fee-paying establishment, you'll find they take
         furniture,
pinching a chair, a small cupboard (if you have such
         things of your own),
a dishonest night-nurse will take any trinket of silver,
even the silver-framed small photo of a wife or a
         husband.
Life must go on, they agree. If you can no longer see
         them, what good are they to *you*?

The Pope and I

(Tune: 'The Sun Whose Rays' – *The Mikado*)

The Pope, whose face,
with robes and lace,
   brings such joy to the Faithful,
could never be
charisma-free
   or horrid, hard or scatheful!
Or hide his light
by day or night
   under a bush or bushel –
it will shine high
and reach the sky,
   proud as the Hindu Kush'll!

I mean to be *The* Bard
   before I die –
we really work quite hard,
   the Pope and I!

I've been on stage★
and on the page,
   and he has written plays too –
infallible
with every Bull,
   he's had his share of praise too!
No, we don't shrink
from printer's ink
   we're, each of us, a writer –
we share that crown
on field and town
   shines brighter than a mitre!

We're intellectual,
   we're no small fry,
we're truly on the ball,
   the Pope and I!

★ A one-act opera *Tobermory* (1979) with music by John Gardner.

Love in a Valley★

Valkyrie's Valspeak in Awesome Valhalla

I used to think Wotan was vicious
in all that gear, a real soc, a mega hunk

We flew high, a bitchen sesh,
it was radical!

Those pointy things on his helmet
were truly gnarly, the Heinies were
tubular.
And the Lowies.

Totally!

The bud was caj
we scarfed out. It was hot.
He maxed OK

OK!
How come he get so gross?
such a zod, so nerdy?
a shanky spaz?

OK!
Now I wanta say:

Gag me with a spoon!
What a geek!
You were mondo cool
but now you're grody
you make me barf
you're not buf any more . . .

Oh my God!
Kiss my tuna!
What a nerd!
Get away!
Your fat butt disgusts me!

★ Spoken, as it were, by a Valley Girl in Los Angeles, living in or
near the San Fernando Valley.

The Inventor of Franglais?

A Comment

Thence to Jervas's, my mind, God forgive me, running too much after sa fille, but elle not being within, I away by coach to the Change – and thence home to dinner; and finding Mrs. Bagwell waiting at the office after dinner, away elle and I to a cabaret where elle and I have été before; and there I had her company toute l'après-diner and had mon plein plaisir of elle – but strange, to see how a woman, notwithstanding her greatest pretences of love à son mari and religion, may be vaincue.

– Samuel Pepys, Diary (23 January 1665)

Well, God, j'ai souvent pensé
(in clear or fractured français),
a pris the soul of femmes –
but toutefois the Devil maudit
is souverain of their body
and has his will of Dames!

He does all that he voulait
to each partridge or poulet,
we're instruments – c'est tout!
Bon Dieu, above, has thunder –
le Diable rules what's under –
très bon for me and you!

Les female protestations
qui annoncent their detestations
of all luxurieux men
sont for the record only,
le corps stays soft and lonely
et le fait again et again!

The Importance of Being Earnest

Jack Worthing is free, fit and fine –
and he knows about women and wine.
Less coarse than a sandbag,
he was found in a *handbag* –
on the Brighton, that famous old line.

Algy Moncrieff does a Bunbury
to places like Paris or Sunbury –
to see a sick friend
who is nearing his end –
but in truth he's at Joysville or Funbury!

There are two girls: Gwendolen, Cecily,
who go round full of wit, and quite dressily.
Lady Bracknell's the Aunt –
not her fault that it shan't
end in tears and in all ways quite messily!

C.'s governess, prune-faced Miss Prism,
Canon Chasuble; heresy, schism
fly away when *he's* there.
She'd be willing to share
any fate as his mate – cataclysm!

Now Jack's told one lie or another,
told Cecily he has a brother
called Ernest – who's wicked –
this isn't quite cricket
(no one knows yet who might be his mother).

So the Albany country-house lads
must endure the girls' maidenly fads –
C.'s a chick who in *her* nest
wants no one not Ernest.
Ditto Gwendolen. *Christen us cads*!

is the favour they both of them ask,
it's the Canon's canonical task.
But – one last catechism –
Lady B. questions Prism,
and the Truth is revealed, with no mask!

That (how fateful and how well-arranged!)
for a *novel* the young Jack was changed
by Miss Prism, his nurse,
and for better or worse
he's the brother of Alg., long estranged!

Even better, his true given name
will revive the young Cecily's flame!
For it's Ernest (no catch!),
so it's game, set and match
(and the winner was wit in that game)!

Two Kiplings

1 Sixty-seven and going West

When your hair gets thin and your tummy expands
and the frog-spots play all over your hands,
when benign skin-cancers cover your back
and warts, all over, are on the attack –
why, then you'll know (if you haven't guessed)
that you're sixty-seven and going West!

When your face gets fat with a jowly jaw
and your teeth feel like a neglected saw,
when your legs walk easily into cramp,
and your eyes grow tired in the reading lamp –
why, then you'll know (if you haven't guessed)
that you're sixty-seven and going West!

When you feel arthritis in finger-ends
and the stiffness of Death lays out your friends,

when the hand writes wobbly and memory goes
and your hearing weakens, from head to toes
you'll have the *proof* (if you haven't guessed)
that you're sixty-seven and going West!

2 John Kipling

(posted missing in 1915, aged seventeen)

Warned against women, he went off to war,
Dad's most treasured cub in the whole Wolf Pack,
Abraham's Isaac – but where was the ram?

Trained to kiss rods, to kiss and adore,
He never would blub, he was white, not black,
He had a little bread – but never any jam.

Fairly High Windows

(based on an idea of Vernon Scannell's)

They fuck you up, your King and Queen.
    They may not mean to, but they do.
And things that are no way your scene
    All have to be extolled by you.

They have a strict and soppy code
    That never bends much or relents.
Each Royal Birth's a fucking Ode
    And camp as any row of tents.

The Laureate misery's handed down,
    Letters from fools too, sack by sack.
You have to wear that iron crown.
    You're not allowed to give it back.

NOTE   *Written in expectation of Philip Larkin achieving
the Laureateship, June 1984.*

130

Drinker to Lover, Drunkard to Lecher

A glass of wine
won't say *No!*
or *Don't!* or *Let me go!*
You won't be asked
by any jar:
Who do you think you are?
You'll never hear
from pints of bitter
the hard words of a baby-sitter . . .

No double gin
answers back –
it hasn't got the knack –
it can't look pert,
annoyed or coy –
You're not my kind of boy
is something it
will never answer –
or yet *You're not much of a dancer!*

A vodka's smooth,
can be neat,
and vermouths can be very sweet –
they don't avoid
encroaching lips
or smack your fingertips.
They know their place,
won't fail to meet you,
and know exactly how to treat you!

Mr Ewart

Mr Ewart won't answer letters,
Mr Ewart is old and tired,
he is fed up with his betters
and his worses aren't admired.

Mr Ewart would like to founder
like an ancient worn-out ship
where the fathoms all sleep sounder
than the flake-outs on a trip.

Mr Ewart would like to vanish
with a minimum of fuss
either womanish or mannish,
or be run down by a bus.

Mr Ewart won't speak to people,
he is deaf, his eyes aren't good,
his response is now so feeble
you know he hasn't understood.

Mr Ewart is antisocial
and is quite opposed to fun,
all he knows is that much woe shall
come upon us – one by one.

Mr Ewart is sick of living,
he'd like quietly to lie down,
return the gifts that God is giving –
and get to Hell out of this town!

The Joys of Surgery

(dedicated to Richard Selzer, author of *Mortal Lessons*)

There's the riot and the rut –
when you make that first clean cut!
As the scarifying scalpel
makes you higher than an Alp'll –
blood appears in pretty beads,
that thin line directly leads
to the laid-bare opal fat,
you feel randy as a rat
and you don't lose much momentum
when you see the gauze omentum!

What's more horny than a heart
heaving with the surgeon's art?
and the clicking of the clips
is a series of short trips,
you're turned on, lit up, elationed –
quite as knocked out as the patient!
The abdomen's Aladdin's Cave
makes you want to rant and rave,
intestines, serpents of Old Nile,
curve and coil – you have to smile –
and you give a tender shiver
at the dark joy of the liver,
while the pink peritoneum,
lovely as an Art Museum,
strikes you with desire and dumb
till you very nearly come . . .

God made this delightful chasm
for your own intense orgasm!

An English Don Wants to Go

Do I want to go to
that big crooked country
where the girls say
You don't know shit –
but you're kinda cute!
Do I want to go?

Yes, I want to go to
that amazing oil-rich country,
where the kids play
with bum and tit
and they're gonna shoot –
yes, I want to go!

Where my clipt, affected
English utterance
goes with the big stiff
old upper lip –
and I'm kinda mute,
with my English utterance!

Where entry's effected
by high-class utterance,
high as a cliff,
with a horsey clip –
and the campus will salute
my most English utterance!

The Owl Writes a Detective Story

A stately home where doves, in dovecotes, coo –
fields where calm cattle stand and gently moo,
trim lawns where croquet is the thing to do.
This is the ship, the house party's the crew:
Lord Feudal, hunter of the lion and gnu,
whose walls display the heads of not a few,

Her Ladyship, once Ida Fortescue,
who, like his Lordship very highborn too
surveys the world with a disdainful moue.
Their son – most active with a billiard cue –
Lord Lazy (stays in bed till half past two).
A Balkan Count called Popolesceru
(an ex-Dictator waiting for a coup).
Ann Fenn, most English, modest, straight and true,
a very pretty girl without a sou.
Adrian Finkelstein, a clever Jew.
Tempest Bellairs, a beauty such as you
would only find in books like this (she'd sue
if I displayed her to the public view –
enough to say men stick to her like glue).
John Huntingdon, who's only there to woo
(a fact, except for her, the whole house knew)
Ann Fenn. And, last, the witty Cambridge Blue,
the Honourable Algy Playfair, who
shines in detection. His clear 'View halloo!'
puts murderers into a frightful stew.

But now the plot unfolds! What *déjà vu*!
There! In the snow! – The clear print of a shoe!
Tempest is late for her next rendez-vous,
Lord Feudal's blood spreads wide – red, sticky goo
on stiff white shirtfront – Lazy's billet-doux
has missed Ann Fenn, and Popolesceru
has left – without a whisper of adieu
or saying goodbye, typical *mauvais gout*!
Adrian Finkelstein, give him his due,
behaves quite well. Excitement is taboo
in this emotionless landowner's zoo.
Algy, with calm that one could misconstrue
(handling with nonchalance bits of vertu)
knows who the murderer is. He has a clue.

But who? But who? Who, who, who, who, who, who?

NOTE *This poem was written to be read aloud, and the*
'oo' sounds at the ends of the lines should be intoned like the
call of an owl.

Notes

Page

12   *Audenesque For An Initiation*   One of the best poems in Auden's first book was in this metre (the metre of Tennyson's "Locksley Hall"). J. C. Squire was a rather over-hearty cricket-playing poet and editor. A Fifteen is a Rugby Football team.

17   *John Betjeman's Brighton*   Lord Alfred Douglas (downfall of Oscar Wilde) lived in Brighton in the Thirties. The "machines of shame" were hand-cranked peepshows. You put a penny in and turned the handle, to see fan-dancers and moustachioed gentlemen with ladies — all a bit Ninetyish. The knickers are the panties (or bloomers) worn by the naughty ladies. "Fuller's layer-cake". Fuller's tea-shops specialized in this famous cake (a sponge-cake covered with white icing and with walnuts in the mixture and on top — it was delicious). Hove is the genteel part of Brighton, to the West, once a separate town. The Lawns are part of the Promenade, overlooking the sea.

20   *When A Beau Goes In*   This poem is written, roughly, in the Royal Air Force slang of the Forties. A "Beau" is a Beaufighter, the standard twin-engined night-fighter used by the British. "Going in" simply means "going into the drink (the sea)". Crashing on land was called "hitting the deck". "Going for a Burton" means being killed, or being "missing" — inspired by a wartime poster for Burton's Ales. An empty seat at the table, and the caption: "Where's Joe?" Answer: "He's gone for a Burton!" The "land where falls no rain nor hail, etc." is Tennyson's Avilion in the "Morte d'Arthur".

26   *Crossing The Bar*   A re-vamping of Tennyson's famous poem, with the same title. Katie, in the 1960's, was the housewife who claimed (in television ads) that Oxo (dehydrated gravy sold in cubes) gave her meals "Man Appeal". Bournvita was a chocolate-flavoured nightcap drink, a rival to Horlick's. The "gamekeeper's cottage in the woods" is from *Lady Chatterley's Lover.*

23   *In and Out the Dusty Bluebells*   A children's singing and dancing game. The Atom Bomb (as it was in the Sixties) is the background threat.

25 *A Christmas Message* "Epitaxial planar techniques" — very advanced in the Sixties — were the techniques involved in the miniaturisation of circuitry. "Rationalized packaging" is, similarly, the technique of compressing circuitry or other components into a small space. Bass is a famous beer. The Peloponnese is part of Ancient Greece. "Autochthonous" means indigenous, "sprung from the soil" (the Athenians even had a grasshopper as their emblem, to make this point).

35 *Arithmetic* The "Rec" is a children's Recreation Ground, with swings, etc. The girl speaking is what we would now call a "latchkey" child.

38 *Ella mi fu rapita!* ("She was taken from me!"), the cry of the wicked Duke of Mantua in Verdi's *Rigoletto*, when Gilda has been kidnapped by the courtiers. The quotation from Brecht's *Dreigroschenoper* means "Love lasts or doesn't last".

42 *The Sentimental Education* "Dadie" is George Rylands, "Anthony" is Anthony Blunt, then young Fellows of King's and Trinity Colleges respectively. Richards is I. A. Richards, inventor of Practical Criticism and Basic English. Leavis, who was my "supervisor", is the well-known critic F. R. Leavis. Tambi = Tambimuttu (editor of *Poetry London*). Nicholas Moore (poet) and Helen Scott were his assistants. The "Beaver" is Lord Beaverbrook (his Fleet Street nickname), proprietor of *The Daily Express* and a Philistine opponent of the British Council. William Hill is a famous bookmaker. An E-type is a Jaguar sports car. "After Eight" — brand name of a much advertised after-dinner chocolate mint.

47 *To A Plum-Coloured Bra Displayed in Marks & Spencer.* Marks & Spencer have a chain of stores all over Britain, selling clothes and (now) food and drink.

50 *The Larkin Automatic Car Wash* Written as a 'para-poem' to Philip Larkin's "The Whitsun Weddings", in the days when Car Washes were very new, using the same rhyme-scheme, the same number of stanzas, it also describes a journey and has a vaguely mystical experience as its conclusion. This is not a humorous poem or a parody.

52 *Trafalgar Day, 1972* The 21st October, when Nelson was killed on board his flag-ship *The Victory* in 1805, after defeating the French. He had only one eye and only one arm. A "one-armed bandit" is the fruit machine beloved by gamblers. Nelson, egged on by Lady Hamilton and the horrible Queen of Naples, summarily executed captured Republican leaders, notably Admiral Caracciolo.

55 *The Hut* The Slade Art School is very famous in Britain.

57 *The Theory of the Leisure Class* Title of a book by Thorsten Veblen. The phrase about "pious frauds" is from a novel by Wilkie Collins. Mr. Mantalini is a very affected character in Dickens who spoke like this.

61 *Is There Life After Sex?* "Fucate". The "fucus" was the thick layer of make-up ladies used to apply to their faces in the 17th Century. "Bilocation" is being in two places at once, possible only for Roman Catholic Saints. A "double crown poster" is the smaller size poster displayed on London Underground stations.

66 *To Lord Byron* Written in the stanza Byron used for *Don Juan*. Miss Chaworth was an early aristocratic girlfriend. Mrs. Whitehouse is a Puritan censor (self-appointed) of improper words and actions transmitted on television.

67 *The Gentle Sex (1974)* This poem is written in the stanza invented by Gerard Manley Hopkins for *The Wreck of the Deutschland*. Like his poem, it is based on a newspaper article (the account of the trial). UDA is the Ulster Defence Association, a Protestant activist body. Long Kesh is the main prison in Belfast. The Loyalists believe that Northern Ireland should continue to remain part of Britain.

72 *"The lion griefs, etc."* These lines are from one of Auden's greatest poems, written in June 1933 and once called "Summer Night". It begins "Out on the lawn I lie in bed".

77 *The Semantic Limerick* This is Semantic Poetry, invented by Stefan Themerson in 1945 (in his novel *Bayamus*). The words in a poem are replaced by their dictionary definitions.

87 *A Contemporary Film of Lancasters in Action* Lancasters were the 4-engined bombers used by the R.A.F. in the later stages of the 1939-45 War.

90 *On First Looking Into Michael Grant's 'Cities of Vesuvius'* Michael Grant's admirable book is about the eruption of 79 A.D., when Pompeii, Herculaneum and Stabiae (now Castellamare) were covered by hot ash, lava or volcanic mud. The poem is in hexameters, befitting its Classical subject.

106 *Aros Castle* The castle is a ruin on the East coast of the Island of Mull, off the West coast of Scotland. *Present Indicative* was the first book of autobiography by Noel Coward. Margery (Turner) was one of my mother's cousins.

128 *The Importance of Being Earnest* A limerick version of Oscar Wilde's famous comedy. "Bunbury" was the imaginary relative, to visit whose sickbed Algy Moncrieff used to be called

away — in reality he would be enjoying himself in, for example, Dieppe or Paris.

130   *Fairly High Windows*   A parody. The first line was supplied by Vernon Scannell. The original poem, "This Be The Verse", begins "They fuck you up, your Mum and Dad" and appears in *High Windows* (1974). As it turned out, Ted Hughes was appointed Poet Laureate.